Asylum—A Moral Dilemma

Asylum—A Moral Dilemma

W. Gunther Plaut

York Lanes Press
Toronto

Canadian Cataloguing-in-Publication Data

Plaut, W. Gunther, 1912 –
    Asylum

Includes bibliographical references and index.
ISBN 1-55014-239-9

1. Asylum, Right of.
2. Refugees — Legal status, laws, etc.
I. Title.

K3230.R45P53   1995   342'.083   C95–931584–5

Published by
York Lanes Press, Inc.
Centre for Refugee Studies
York University
North York ON M3J 1P3
Canada

Published in the United States of America by Praeger Publishers, CT.

Cover photo credit: UNHCR/Moumtzb
Cover design by P. Sasiharan

Printed in Canada by University of Toronto Press Inc.

Contents

On a Personal Note

When Howard Adelman, Director of the Centre for Refugee Studies and Professor of Philosophy at York University, asked me to undertake a study of the moral dimensions of refugee issues, I quickly consented. There were several reasons why his request found me ready, but I will mention only two. To begin with, I was a refugee myself, back in the days of the Nazis. Their racial policies brought my law career to an end and caused my family and me to find our way as strangers in strange lands. As it turned out, we were the fortunate ones; so many others, among them uncles, aunts and cousins, became victims of racial madness and perished in the gas chambers of Auschwitz and Treblinka.

In fact, the experience of the Jewish people in their long history may be seen as a paradigm of what happens or may happen to strangers. Jews began their trek through history as outsiders in Egypt in the second millennium B.C.E. In the succeeding centuries up to modern times they were refugees time and again, and lived as strangers in many lands. Their Bible, replete with laws and pleadings concerning the treatment of strangers, helped to shape the sensibilities of Christianity and Western culture, as well as of Islam and its wide spiritual and temporal influence.

Second, refugee law had become familiar to me ever since the Canadian government asked me, in 1984, to make a study of the refugee determination process. In the course of the investigation, I travelled across the country and consulted with refugees as well as with legal and political authorities, analysts, and advocates in Canada and in the United States and a number of European nations.

Not surprisingly, the literature on refugees is enormous, and every day brings new publications. My thanks go to authors and publishers who allowed me to cite passages from their books, papers and addresses.

Special words of gratitude are extended to Natalie Fingerhut for imaginatively assisting me in my research; to my secretary, Deborah Tameanko, for helping to persuade the word processor to do our bidding; and to the staff of the Centre for Refugee Studies at York University and those associated with its important work. Special thanks to Erika Krolman for her many perceptive suggestions, and to Arul Aruliah of York Lanes Press for patiently guiding the book through the publication process.

Summer of '94, Toronto, Canada.

Man's moral sense is not a strong beacon light, radiating outward to illuminate in sharp outline all that it touches. It is, rather, a small candle flame, casting vague and multiple shadows, flickering and sputtering in the strong winds of power and passion, greed and ideology. But brought close to the heart and cupped in one's hands, it dispels the darkness and warms the soul.

—*James Q. Wilson*

The road of the refugee is as long as you make it.

—*United Nations High Commissioner for Refugees*

Abbreviations

B.C.E.	Before the Common Era
C.E.	Common Era
INS	Immigration and Naturalization Service (U.S.A.)
IRB	Immigration and Refugee Board (Canada)
NGO	Non-government organization
OAU	Organization of African Unity
PLO	Palestine Liberation Organization
TPS	Temporary Protected Status (U.S.A.)
UNHCR	United Nations High Commissioner for Refugees

PART ONE:

The Issues

1

Questions Without Answers

Raising Questions

Every year the refugee landscape changes, but only in that more problems are added, fewer are solved, and all become constantly more urgent.

This study attempts to look at the way ethical concerns impact on the refugee scene. In so doing it encounters a fundamental dilemma: the clash of a nation's real or perceived interests on the one side, and the needs of refugees on the other. In this clash, power is distributed unevenly: nations have it and refugees do not, except for the moral claim they make. Thus, the internal and external *realpolitik* of the state confronts the basic desire of human beings for a decent life. The distinguishing mark of these people is that they come from the outside and are not part of a citizenry that shapes a nation's policies.

Whatever their attitude towards needful outsiders may be, states will insist that their actions have a sound ethical basis, that is, they must account not only for the needs of refugees but also those of their own people. This clash of interests resists easy solutions because both sides claim high moral ground—the stuff of a classic dilemma. It is the very nature of dilemmas that they may not and often will not allow clear-cut solutions.

This book aims at raising questions and outlining the debates that surround this conundrum. It tries to survey a fairly new field in which old problems of moral behaviour focus on refugee matters. The consideration of these issues is open-ended and does not advance one particular point of view. Rather, its goal is to involve the reader in much-needed discussion. It raises questions rather than providing answers.

Still, this writer does have a distinct objective: he hopes that, when the issues are considered with care, those who understand them will lead others to greater generosity when it comes to formulating solutions that are both pragmatic and moral.

A Need for Asylum

The approaching twenty-first century will be characterized by two phenomena. One is the explosion of the world's population, which presently stands at five billion and shows no signs of slowing its rate of growth. The social, political, environmental, and economic consequences of unchecked human proliferation are self-evident, and realistic solutions are not in sight.

The second feature of the next century will be an almost exponential increase in migration. According to a 1993 United Nations report,

> international migration has reached unprecedented levels and could become the human crisis of our age ... In 1989, the UN estimated that some 50 million people, or one percent of the world population, lived in a country other than their country of origin. In 1992, the World Bank estimated international migrants of all kinds at 100 million ... Family unification has been a major influence on the composition of flows in recent years. Increasing numbers of workers and undocumented migrants have raised the proportion of unskilled workers. The impact of international migration is far greater than the figures suggest. Numbers are substantially greater than reported; migrants are often in the peak years of fertility; migrants tend to concentrate in a few areas, increasing their visibility and the perception of cultural differences ...[1]

Whereas migratory movements formerly were seen as enlarging the development of the host country, today they are perceived as a threat to its security and well-being. This is especially true for that portion of migrants identified (by conventions of various kinds) as refugees.

Larger and larger numbers are in flight, searching for societies they can join, for space where they can realize their basic human aspirations. The latest estimate of refugees in the world is 17.5 million,[2] and there are over 24 million internally displaced persons.[3] There is no question that somehow organized humanity must find a way to deal with these groups constructively and humanely.

Even for those who have occupied themselves with the problems of refugees, the variety of countries producing displaced persons and the large numbers of people in search of new homes is staggering. Add the historic changes that have taken place since the publication of the above study—events subsequent to the dissolution of the Soviet empire, the intra-German migrations after the dismantling of the Berlin Wall, the dissolution of Yugoslavia and the Serb/Bosnian/Croatian war—and the dismal picture grows even darker.

In his introduction to *Refugees in the Age of Total War* (1988), Michael R. Marrus considers the refugee problem to be growing yet finds the global response to be either helplessness or despair over any long-term prospect for a plausible solution. In addition, after the 1950s, the refugees have been primarily Africans, Asians and Middle Eastern peoples rather than Europeans, which has complicated their acceptance in Western industrialized nations.

Marrus lists four factors that have adversely affected the position of the refugees:

1. Nationalist ideologies according to which refugees are a threat to a nation's security, cultural cohesion, or way of life;
2. In a revolutionary age, refugees are carriers of ideas that appear to threaten the host nation's interests (communism, anarchism, etc.);
3. Fear of refugees in terms of national health;
4. Civilians are the main sufferers in an age when war is no longer restricted to battling armies (Marrus 1988, 3ff).

International outcry over invasions or wars has occasionally produced positive responses to the needs of refugees. Thus, the Soviet invasion of Hungary in 1956 resulted in doors in North America being opened to Hungarian refugees. Similarly, the displacements caused by the intra-Yugoslavian conflict in 1992–93 opened some doors for those in flight. But these were small numbers compared to the total human need, which has also increased because it is no longer only war but also hunger and natural disasters that drive people to seek new homes.

State and Individual

For the purposes of this study it seems futile to maintain the rigid distinctions of the UN Refugee Convention (cited in Appendix C). When we inquire into moral/ethical foundations for accepting refugees, legal niceties cannot be meaningfully maintained in the twenty-first century. Other conceptions will have to take their place. Above all, individual countries will not be able to cope with the enormity of the problem. Only a global strategy buttressed by moral considerations can face that task effectively.

International conventions and bodies of national legislation are in place to deal with refugee flows, but somehow the response of many nations, especially those that call themselves developed, has been less and less forthcoming. Border controls are being tightened, legal mechanisms are being set up to reduce the arrival of "unwanted strangers," and every nation loudly proclaims its right to control whom it wishes to admit and whom to exclude.

Against these putative rights of nations are set the rights of human beings to live in an environment free from fear and terror. Every religion recognizes the humanity of all people and accords them respect and dignity. Yet, in the tension between national and individual rights, the former wins out almost invariably, for the nation possesses power while the individual is reduced to beggary at the gate.

Where then are the standards by which the self-interest of nations as well as the needs of refugees can be accommodated? Are there in fact moral foundations for answering this question?

Quite obviously, an asymmetry exists between the rights of states and the rights of persons. States do not have to explain themselves, while personal rights have to be constantly reinforced. Yet there is also a growing recognition that in human relations power is not everything. Moral forces are standing their ground. This book is a study of how the needs of refugees are related to moral concepts, and how the relationship between the two may affect the will and politics of nations.

Refugee Shutdown

Tomasz Kozlowski, Polish Deputy Minister of the Interior, assessed the current crises of refugees and immigrants in Europe as they affect his country:

> For the West, Poland is a buffer against a flood from the East. This is not a role any country should serve for others. We are not the West's immigration office.[4]

Many observers see the fear of immigration and refugees replacing the former fear of nuclear war. In Europe, there were 560,000 asylum seekers in 1992, which represents an almost tenfold increase in one decade. Add to this figure some two million immigrants and an estimated five million illegals, and the urgency of the problem becomes clear. Terrab Mouhcine, governor of Morocco's Tetouan district, looking at the problem from his perspective, said, "Let's manage this flow instead of creating antagonisms and blaming everything on immigration. Europe is closing down on itself."[5]

The closing down of which Mouhcine speaks can be easily documented. The introduction of the "first safe country" principle[6] has spread and threatens to make Europe—or at least the heart of it—refugee-proof. It is likely that the members of the European Community will adopt this principle and that its neighbours will then have to shoulder the responsibility for dealing with an ever-increasing refugee flow. One "solution" is being talked about more and more: each country which is itself safe and serves as its neighbours' dumping place will declare such neighbours "safe" countries.

Thus, in 1993, Austria—which is safe from the German vantage point—stopped admitting Bosnians who were headed for Germany, because they arrived via safe Slovenia, having crossed safe Croatia on the way. (Canada, too, has a safe-country clause on its books, but for the time being has not used it.)

Another "solution" being talked about is that of rejecting the safe-country principle altogether and refusing to accept returnees from countries that want to expel their asylees. The problem this would cause has, of course, been demonstrated many times, albeit on a smaller scale: the number of "refugees in orbit" would swell to unmanageable numbers.

The only ones who benefit from this sordid conundrum are those who smuggle illegal aliens into other countries. Almost inevitably the human toll is gruesomely large. For example, 1,000 asylum seekers died on their way from Morocco to Gibraltar in 1992, when their flimsy boats capsized.

In all of this, compassion and moral consideration seem to be reserved for individuals and religiously based rescue operations. But their numbers are small, and wider success is becoming ever more difficult to achieve.

Immigrants and refugees in 1993 Europe have thus highlighted the clash between high-sounding principles and the public's fear of what foreigners would do to their economy and their national identity. Morality has never functioned in a vacuum, but the current impasse has made it doubly important to point out that amidst all the confusion and difficulties, and the displacements and the wars that bring them about, there is still a small but potent force called the moral law.

Tracing some of its roots, and there are many, is the purpose of this study. It does not aim to provide theoretical or practical means for solving the refugee crisis, but rather to inject the element of moral vision into what has become an immoral morass.

Where Will Refugees Go?

In the history of humanity the term *refugee* is fairly new.[7] As little as a hundred years ago, the specific class of people we now call refugees rarely had trouble finding a place where they could rebuild their lives. During much of the nineteenth century most of the inhabited areas of the world were open to newcomers,[8] whether they were economic, political, or religious refugees. It is the dubious distinction of the twentieth century to be known—in addition to its many achievements—for the concept of closed borders. This in turn has led to the introduction of a variety of national and international laws that deal with refugees in this new environment of inhospitality. And if the twentieth century laid the groundwork for dealing with refugee problems, what can the new century hold in store, given that the problems will enlarge enormously and be ever more urgent? With fewer solutions in the offing, the pressures created by refugees will become more volatile and thereby threaten ever wider areas.

This study is not an exhortation to adopt certain policies; rather, it tries to explore the intersection between various kinds of rights and the role that moral considerations have played and might play. We shall look at the nature of rights and, specifically, at human rights, how history has dealt with problems of asylum and population movements, and how national traditions have made themselves felt when these problems were being confronted and their solutions devised.

Since this study considers global issues, its examples constitute an eclectic survey rather than any in-depth examination. However, special emphasis is laid on Western nations, most of which find themselves in the enviable position of being "developed." It is in the developed nations that the question of moral responsibility is increasingly being raised, for they are the goal of many refugees in flight.

The ongoing flux of refugees defies definitive statements, and this imposes inherent shortcomings on its investigation. The result of the efforts presented here may be seen as a momentary halting place where we consider both the plight and the potential of refugees, as well as their claim on us in settled societies, wherever they may be. The Hebrew Bible reminds us that "Where there is no vision the people perish."[9] Moral concepts are part of that vision.

A Metaphor

As a way of observing the anniversary date of the American bombing of Nagasaki, *The Globe and Mail* in 1992 featured an article entitled "The life-boat dilemma," written by Hazel Strouts, writing from Hiswa, Yemen.

When I have pictured the classic 'life-boat' dilemma in my mind's eye, I have always imagined a neat sea-worthy vessel being tossed about in turbulent seas near a sinking ship. The choice facing those in the life-boat is clear: They can either pull the drowning people on board, which would overload the life-boat and cause everyone to perish, or they can beat the flailing swimmers over the head with oars so that those already on board would be safe.

But the life-boat dilemma, as it unfolds in Yemen, is not like this at all. On the coast of the Gulf of Aden, one of the poorest regions of one of the poorest countries of the world, about 55,000 refugees have arrived from Somalia. Just walking through Hiswa or Madinat al Shaab, two crowded refugee tent cities about twelve kilometers west of the point city of Aden, gives some idea of how bad things must be in Somalia. Some 12,000 Somalis have chosen to stay in these camps under the care of the United Nations High Commissioner for Refugees rather than remain at home.

This particular refugee crisis began with the overthrow of Somali president Mohammed Siad Barre in January 1991, adding violence to already existing famine conditions. Thirty-thousand people were killed in the fighting and the estimate is that currently 1.5 million of the nation's 8 million people are in danger of starving. The hesitant and piecemeal aid by the UN has done little to stem the flow of people who are fleeing their country.

Thousands more escape across the Gulf of Aden to Yemen. Here in the refugee tent cities, the temperature is well over 40 degrees and the humidity is 100 per cent. Sand blows everywhere (at Hiswa at the beach, the air is filled with salt-sand). Monsoon winds strong enough to blow over lamp posts in Aden cause havoc with flapping tents ... So Yemen, the life-boat, takes them on board. Perhaps the people already in the life-boat have little choice. Perhaps they do not have the strength to keep them out. Or perhaps they recognize themselves in these newcomers. Yemenis know what it is like to have next to nothing. Their per capita income is $520 a year. Life expectancy is 46.3 years. Of 1,000 children, 190 die in their first five years ... U.S. Aid officials at Sana'a say that the Somali refugees are, in terms of their health, better off than the average Yemeni because they receive free basic medical attention. "Yemeni children," says Dr. Sugule, "are born at one of the fastest rates in the world, and they die at one of the fastest."

So this is the shipwreck. So these are the life-boats.[10]

Strouts's metaphor focuses on the heart of this sorry tale, a moral dilemma that needs to be faced. There are no simple answers when it comes to refugees.

Notes

1. *The Globe and Mail,* June 22, 1993, A8. The report originally appeared in the *State of the World's Population,* Toronto: Penguin Books, 1993.

2. *World Refugee Survey,* U.S. Committee for Refugees, 1993, 51.

3. Ibid., 52. Information on internal displacement is fragmentary: figures are estimates and no accurate tools are available.

4. *The Globe and Mail,* July 9, 1993.

5. Ibid.

6. According to this principle, the first country where the refugee is safe from persecution should process his/her application for refugee status.

7. For more on its history, see Chapter 2.

8. Exceptions were some closed societies, like China and Japan.

9. Proverbs 29:18.

10. *The Globe and Mail,* August 8, 1992.

2

Definitions

"Asylum"

Asylum is a term which, in the context of this study, signifies refuge offered by a country. In the past, particular places served that function, such as an altar, a temple or church, a city or a ship. Today asylum generally indicates a nation where a refugee may find temporary or permanent shelter.[1]

The word is younger than its concept and practice. It has its origin in the Greek language and culture and is derived from the verb *asylao*, meaning to violate or lay waste. The adjective *asylos/asylon* represents the opposite, namely, inviolable.

Yet the concept was already known in earlier days and probably in prehistoric times as well. It is attested to in many lands and continents, from the Hebrews and pre-Islamic Arabs of the ancient Middle East to the Aztecs of the New World.[2] The Hebrew word *miqlat* describes special cities set aside for asylum or refuge; Oedipus and Theseus of Greek tradition sought and were granted asylum; the New Testament tells of Jesus and his family as refugees who were accepted in Egypt; and Mohammed fled to Abyssinia and, later, to Medina for refuge.

Hospitality is a variant of asylum. But while asylum is today circumscribed and regulated by international and national laws, hospitality remains an expression of character, attitude and tradition rather than of law.

Thus, Sophocles, in *Oedipus at Colon*, has Theseus, King of Thebes, say:

> Like you, I will remember that I grew up in the home of others, and in a foreign land I faced deadly dangers. So that, whoever asks my hospitality as you do now, I would not know how to turn away. In future you will stay here in safety, like me.

In general usage, "asylum" (like *miqlat*) once denoted temporary refuge, but that has changed. For countries adjacent to refugee-producing areas (such as Thailand and Pakistan), "asylum" has in effect come to mean the permanent hosting of refugees.

"Nonrefoulement"

The obligation not to return refugees to the country where they would suffer punishment or persecution is called the principle of *nonrefoulement* (from the French *refouler*, to turn back). The question of whether or not a refugee should be returned was already part of the Hebrew Bible and part of an old Hittite-Egyptian treaty.[3]

"Refugee"

Derived from the French *réfugié*, the word *refugee* was used originally to refer (like its French model) to Protestant Huguenots expelled from France after the Edict of Nantes was abolished by Louis XIV in 1685.[4] For some time, it continued to be used to mean Huguenots, but its meaning eventually expanded from its original, particular sense into a general term denoting people who had left their home country due to duress. An early edition of the *Encyclopaedia Britannica* noted that this usage was then current, pointing out: "In Germany, where many of the Huguenots fled, the existing word *Flüchtling* (a person who flees) assumed the additional meaning of Huguenots."[5] According to the *Sachs-Villatte* French dictionary, as late as 1911, this use of the word *réfugié* was current.

Interpretations

"Convention refugees," as defined in the UN Convention of 1951 and its 1967 Protocol, are those who "by reason of a well-founded fear of persecution for reasons of race, religion, nationality, membership in a particular social group or political opinion" have left their country of habitual residence and are unwilling to return there or unable to do so. (For the full definition see Appendix C.) The original document focused on European victims of World War II, but the Protocol made the Convention applicable regardless of place or time.[6]

In the former Soviet countries, the right of asylum was viewed as a "class symptom." The 1976 Constitution of the Soviet Union stated in Article 38:

> The U.S.S.R. grants the right of asylum to foreigners persecuted for defending the interests of the working people and the cause of peace, or for participation in a revolutionary or national liberation movement, or for progressive social and political, scientific, or other creative activity.

A successful applicant for asylum would likely have been active in the noncommunist world by promoting the principles of socialism, but there was—even for such applicants—no individual right to asylum.

A number of African states have treated this issue in a fundamentally different manner and have adopted article 1 of the 1969 OAU Convention, which states:

> The term "refugee" shall ... apply to every person who, owing to external aggression, occupation, foreign domination or events seriously disturbing public order either in part or in whole of his or her country of origin or nationality, is compelled to leave his or her place of habitual residence in order to seek refuge in another place of his or her country of origin or nationality.

This definition is a model for the breadth of its coverage, and various states have made it part of their national legislation. Examples are Burundi, Zimbabwe, Senegal, Lesotho, Tunisia, Gabon and Uganda. But elsewhere as well, there is an increasing tendency to view the refugee model drafted by the OAU as pathbreaking and as a model for the amendment for the current refugee Convention.

Western countries like Canada and the United States generally favour the acceptance of refugees from countries whose policies they do *not* like—in the past it was refugees from communist countries and in such cases it was easy to prove that the applicant had a well-founded fear of persecution. But when persons claim refugee status because of events in their homelands that happen to be allies of or friendly with the Western country in which they seek refuge, they will likely find it difficult to be accepted. Even if they are in serious distress, they may be deemed economic migrants rather than political refugees, and therefore subject to refoulement.[7]

Latin American states at first narrowed the terms of the Geneva Convention. Whereas the latter states that the claimant for protection needs a "well-founded fear of persecution," the 1969 San José Pact defined persecution as occurring when "right to life or personal freedom is in danger of being violated." But in 1984, the Cartagena Declaration broadened the definition of refugee considerably and included those fleeing generalized violence. Created by the governments of the region and the UNHCR (except for the United States), it was a document that approved of a broader definition of refugees: "similar to the one used by the OAU ... It demonstrates the efforts made by Latin American governments to adapt the tradition of asylum to the new conditions of massive displacements" (Larkin, Cuny and Stein 1991, ix; Zolberg, Suhrke and Aguayo 1989, 220ff.; Goodwin-Gill 1988, 103ff.).[8]

Still, despite its shortcomings, the UN definition "remains one of the few human rights standards recognized, and to a degree upheld, by both international bodies and the laws of many nations. We need both to protect it and to seek constantly to make its ideals our reality" (Rubin 1991, 30).

The Moral Dimension

The term *moral*, occurs frequently in this study, and it is therefore best to delimit its usage. *Webster's New International Dictionary* defines "moral" in various ways. Among them are:

> ... of or relating to principles or considerations of right and wrong action or good and bad character;
> ... of or relating to the study of such principles or considerations;
> ... capable of being judged as good or evil or in terms of principles of right and wrong action;
> ... conforming to or proceeding from a standard of what is good and right.

Moral law is defined in the same source as "a general rule of right living; especially such a rule or group of rules conceived as universal and unchanging and as having the sanction of God's will, of conscience, of man's moral nature, or of natural justice as revealed to human reason." In this study "ethical" is treated as a synonym for moral.

Gary E. Rubin (1991, 30) has explained the need to consider the moral implications of immigration and refugee policies:

> No matter how dispassionate, objective or scholarly, *all* work in this field *inevitably* rests on moral principles ... It is impossible to address or even frame questions in this field without the guidance of an ethical value system, even if it is an unconscious one.

"Human Rights"

James W. Nickel (1983, 32ff.) defines *right* as "a high priority prescription of a freedom or benefit that generates definite obligations for parties other than the right holder." It is the nature of these rights that they are inalienable, that is to say that they exist and can be implemented regardless of race, sex, religion, and national and social position, and independently of government—in fact neither government nor individuals can alienate these rights. In consequence of the impotence of the world vis-à-vis the wholesale violation of human rights by the Nazis, the notion that a violation of human rights should warrant international action gained acceptance. Policies and indifference have so far proven to be formidable impediments, however.

Today, commonly accepted standards of human rights, buttressed by international declarations, would include the following categories:

1. Rights to due process, that is, a fair trial and freedom from torture;
2. Rights to personal security, that is, protection from unlawful government incursion and from crime;
3. Rights to personal autonomy, that is, freedom of movement, privacy, freedom of thought and religion;
4. Rights to political participation, that is, the right to vote and speak;
5. Rights to equality, that is, the right to freedom from discrimination and to equality before the law;
6. Economic and social rights, that is, the right to a decent standard of living, education and medical care.[9]

These rights are not dependent on citizenship in any particular country and adhere to humans as such, which is to say that they apply to aliens and especially to refugees.[10]

Notes

1. Occasionally a foreign embassy or the Vatican serve the same purpose on a temporary basis.
2. See the survey by Waldon Villalpando (1991), pp. 35ff.
3. See Chapter 3 and Appendix A.
4. For more on the Huguenots, see Chapter 4.

5. 1769 edition.
6. For fuller citations of international agreements, see Appendices B and C.
7. For details and statistics, see Frelick (1992).
8. For a critical view, see R. Plender (1989).
9. Among the bodies of law that address and define these rights are the Universal Declaration of Human Rights, the International Covenant on Civil and Political Rights, the American Convention on Human Rights, and others.
10. Nickel refers to the International Covenant on Economic, Social and Cultural Rights as not being immediately possible of compliance "because of the high cost of making welfare and medical services available to all" (1983, 33). This reference is not to European or North American countries, but to those host nations that are too poor to implement welfare and medical rights.

3

Religion, Natural Law and Hospitality

The granting of asylum is rooted primarily in religious and secular traditions that often overlap and occasionally clash. All of them relate to human rights, for persons in search of asylum make their claim on the world because of their humanity.

The Hebrew Bible

1. The Stranger

The frequency of the demand to treat the stranger, or *ger*, with kindness and to protect his or her rights must rightly astonish the reader. No other command (except to recognize the supremacy of God) is repeated as often—more than thirty times! This forces us to conclude that there was a need for the admonition to be repeated. The outsider, who did not or could not share in the cultic practices of the host nation, was always the "other" in a fairly homogeneous society, which defined itself by inherited tribal and religious allegiances. Many perceived otherness as a danger to the common weal.

However, it was the distinction of the ancient Hebrews that their legislation (the Torah) tried to balance their desire for cultural and religious cohesion with an injunction against xenophobia and called attention to its roots. The repeated command is: "Do not oppress the stranger, for you know the feeling of the stranger, having yourselves been strangers in the land of Egypt."[1] The Israelites are reminded that the *ger* shares with them a common humanity and that this humanity finds its root in a Divinity that cares for all its children. This conception is pragmatically summarized by the eighth century B.C.E. prophet Amos who has God say to the Israelites: "Are you not like the Ethiopians before Me?"—meaning, I, God, value both of you equally in your common humanity and see no difference between you.[2]

2. Slaves

The Hebrew scriptures establish the principle of nonrefoulement in the case of slaves:

> You shall not turn over to his master a slave who seeks refuge with you from his master. He shall live with you in any place he may choose among the settlements in your midst, wherever he pleases; you must not ill-treat him (Deuteronomy 23:16–17).[3]

While the first verse may suggest that the slave is an *internal* refugee—that is, one who seeks refuge from an Israelite master within the country—the next makes it clear that the slave is an *external* refugee, coming from abroad. For the meaning here is clearly that the slave who has come from another country may choose to live anywhere in Israel. The Aramaic translation by Onkelos confirms this meaning, as does the Babylonian Talmud, which notes that this rule obtained also if the owner abroad was an Israelite.[4] During the nineteenth century, the underground movement of slaves from the American South to its North, and from America in general to Canada, was given moral justification by this ancient legislation.[5]

The religious origins of asylum are in evidence elsewhere in the Hebrew Bible as well. While they refer to internal asylum, it may be assumed that the concept of asylum itself—whether external or internal—finds its rationale in overriding principles enunciated by or ascribed to the Divinity.

3. Cities of Refuge

Chapter 35 of the Book of Numbers provides that a person who killed unintentionally could find security from the blood avenger in one of six designated cities, the *arei miqlat*, "cities of refuge." A trial would then be held in the locale where the slaying had occurred and, if malice aforethought was not established, the manslayer would be sent back to the city of refuge and held there securely until the death of the reigning High Priest.[6]

While the cities-of-refuge institution did not survive the final destruction of the Second Commonwealth in 70 C.E., a second form of internal asylum did: refuge at the sanctuary altar.[7] A direct spiritual descendant of this custom was the sanctuary movement of the 1980s (see Chapter 12).

Christian Traditions

Asylum

Seen through the lens of religion, the foundation of the right of asylum is the divine prerogative that asserts itself over the exercise of human power, and the medieval Christian Church asserted this point repeatedly. It transferred the sacredness of the biblical altar to its own realm and granted the right of asylum to those who sought refuge in churches or monasteries, which, as places dedicated to God, demanded special respect.[8] The practice of church asylum found its most notable expression in Europe from the fifth to the fifteenth centuries. It then waned and disappeared *de facto*, but has not been officially abandoned by the Roman Catholic Church (Kimminich 1968, 87).

Church asylum is different from that described by the Hebrew Bible in that it was extended even to those who acted with intent. Despite abuses of such asylum during the many centuries in which it was practised, the newly revised *Codex Juris Canonici* declares:

> Every Church has the privilege of being a place of asylum, so that the law breakers who flee thither may not be surrendered without the agreement of the priest or church authority unless there is overriding reason to do so.[9]

"The Other"

Mary Jo Leddy (1993), who works with refugees at Romero House in Toronto, expresses her view of the obligation to acknowledge the "otherness" in the stranger:

> I am now convinced that the command of the other lies at the heart of living spiritually with the reality of refugees. All too often, well-intentioned refugee advocates present concerns for refugees as an indication of our moral awareness. This subtly reinforces our position at the center of the moral and political universe. In the culture of the empire, the *I*, even the socially conscious *I* becomes imperial. How blessed we would be if we recognized the arrival of refugees as a time

of visitation. [10] In their very otherness, in their very strangeness, they summon us to a deeper awareness of the scene that grips liberal democracies: the imperialism of the ego. We have so exalted the I, the self, the subject, that we are continually tempted to reduce the rest of the world to the object of our needs and wants, or even to the object of our concern. When we are visited by someone genuinely other than ourselves, someone who is like God, we are tempted to reduce him or her to the status of an object.

Leddy therefore sees the experience of refugees as revealing the contradiction of liberal democracies which have an enlightened view of individual human rights but seem to have difficulty recognizing that others not like us have these same rights.

People who are refugees are caught between these diverse yet similar responses: between those who treat them as objects of moral concern and those who treat them as objects of suspicion. In the process, human beings are defaced.

She recounts how for the last two years she has lived with refugees, because she could not consider working for them without living with them. To her, "refugee" is only one category of concern and cannot sum up the totality of the other's life—a person who is not always a refugee and who will not always be one.

We can no longer treat one another as objects of concern, as "clients," as "causes," as "cases." To allow for the possibility of friendship is to become liberated from the oppressive cultural categories that prevent us from being surprised by joy.

Islamic Sources

Islam's holy scripture, the Quran, deals several times with the protection that is to be extended to strangers. While the Hebrew scriptures appeal to memory as a motivating force for extending protection, the Quran appeals to the missionary impulse:[11]

And if any one of the idolaters seeks your protection, then protect him so that he may hear the word of God and afterward take him to his place of safety (9:6).

The Quran, like the Hebrew Bible, emphasizes that God is the possessor of all the earth and that human beings are only his stewards, not its owners: "[The angels] ask: 'Was not God's earth broad enough for you to migrate from there?' (4:97) ... whoever flees his country for the cause of God, will find on earth many having the same need ... (4:100)."

The Quran also cites the pertinent statement of the Mishnah:[12]"Whoever saves a life it is as though he had saved the lives of all human kind" (Quran 5:32; Mishnah Sanhedrin 4:5).

Islamic tradition has incorporated the demand of hospitality, although it has not formally become part of Islamic law:

> In its practical application, the institution combines elements of the complex system of ties of hospitality to which general opinion seems to assimilate the rights of the *dakhil* [literally interior, inward, intimate, but here referring to a guest to whom protection should be assured, as well as a stranger passing through, or a person of another race], and of a very old law of refuge in private households (acting as shrines) which is attested all over the Semitic world."[13]

The religious protection of holy places is very old, and is traceable to early texts which speak of a person taking asylum in a temple.

Hospitality towards the stranger is also expressed by the term *idjara*. It was a point of honour to protect the *djar* (the person to be protected) as effectively as one protected one's own kin, and shortcoming in this could mean a serious taunt. Normally a request for *djiwar* (protection) had to be accepted (see Quran 9:6), but how long it would last was not covered by any hard or fast rules.[14]

The overarching rule was contained in the Quran:

> So give what is due to kindred, the needy and the wayfarer. That is best for those who seek the countenance of Allah, and it is they who will prosper (30:38).

Buddhist Perception

The idea of Buddha as a refuge is paralleled in other religions. The Hebrew Bible, for instance, speaks of God as a refuge.[15] In Buddhism, however, the refuge becomes a place of liberation from our normal desires and aspirations.

> Becoming a refugee is acknowledging that we are groundless, and it is acknowledging that there is no need for home, or ground. Taking refuge is an expression of freedom, because as refugees we are no longer bounded by the need for security. We are suspended in a no-man's land in which the only thing to do is to relate to the teachings [of Buddha] and with ourselves. (Trungpa 1991, 85)

Here, the teaching of withdrawal from everyday concerns in put into clear relief. The categories of refuge and asylum current in Western or Muslim thought do not seem to apply with the same force.

The Realm of Hinduism

Hinduism describes the civilization of the peoples of the subcontinent of India and is essentially a way of life rather than a set of religious beliefs, though various religions flourish in its realm. According to the *Encyclopaedia Britannica*, "In principle ... Hinduism incorporates all forms of belief and worship without necessitating the selection or elimination of any." It has traditionally fostered acceptance of others, and in its basic pluralism has managed to assimilate and acculturate diverse ideas and national backgrounds.

As a multicultural and pluralistic society (with a large Muslim population), India may be said to be essentially accepting of strangers, among whom refugees from neighbouring countries have often played an important role. The nation has recently during the twentieth century experienced an influx of refugees from Tibet, Sri Lanka, Afghanistan and Pakistan. (See Chapter 10 below.)

Natural Law

The Philosophers

Philosophy scholars generally distinguish between religious and secular perceptions of natural law. The former predominated in Europe during the Middle Ages and was examined thoroughly by Thomas Aquinas; the latter was dominant among the ancient Greeks and Romans and has been preferred since the Renaissance.

While the Romans did not base their approach to natural law on philosophic considerations as did the Greeks, they did develop the concept of *jus gentium*, or law of nations, which they deemed to be applicable to all human beings. The idea was revived in the seventeenth century by a Dutch jurist, Hugo Grotius, who considered the world dominated by a rational law of nature. Human beings, therefore, owed allegiance to this law, which by definition was immutable, and only by following it could people live together in peace, with universal moral standards as their guide.

From this premise arose the idea of a social contract, first outlined by Grotius himself and later developed by Thomas Hobbes, John Locke, Charles Louis Montesquieu and Jean-Jacques Rousseau.[16] While Hobbes derived from the idea of the social contract the need for an authoritarian regime to hold people in line and curb their natural instincts, the majority of natural law philosophers deduced the opposite and found it guaranteed greater protection of individual rights, such as the integrity of the person and property, which they considered fundamental.

In the last two centuries, natural law fell out of favour with philosophers, but it has gained new support after the excesses of twentieth-century fascism and communism. Political theorists maintain that the United Nations Declaration of Universal Rights is an outflow of a broad conception of natural law. While Western nations might have wished to derive the declaration from religious sources, the Soviet Union vigorously opposed this, and a more general formulation was adopted which left the source of law unidentified.

Rights Derived from Natural Law

Religious interpretations of natural law have found their greatest resonance in the Roman Catholic Church, and Jacques Maritain (1958) is its chief modern interpreter.[17] According to Maritain, natural law is "an order or a disposition which human reason can discover and according to which the human will must act in order to attune itself to the necessary ends of the human being" (1958, 35). Natural law is unwritten and exists because it has been inscribed in the very nature of the human personality. As man's moral conscience has developed, so also has the knowledge of natural law.[18]

Human rights derive from our conception of natural law of which they are presumed to be a part. Maritain isolates three basic categories:

1. The *rights of the human person*, to which belong the rights to existence and to property, and the right of every human being to be treated as a person, not as a thing;

2. The *rights of the civic person*, such as political equality, the right to security and liberty, and the equal possibility of admission to public employment and free access to the various professions; and

3. The *rights of the social person*, and more particularly of the working person. They include the right to work, the right to

freely choose one's work (which, for refugees especially, means that they need not necessarily have to work for minimal wages), the right to partake of the elementary goods, material and spiritual, which civilization offers (1958, 60).

What impact do these concepts have on the status of refugees? For instance, if a refugee has the right to safety in another country, but his presence will force a citizen of that other country to starve because there is a shortage of food, whose right has precedence?[19] This type of argument has been adduced in many countries in times of recession, when immigrants and refugees are seen as a threat to the resident population. But as pointed out elsewhere, while in the short run such displacements may and do occur, immigrants and refugees are eventually more likely to enhance the economy of their new-found country.

Two Views

Henry Shue divides natural rights into two classes: basic and nonbasic. He identifies first and foremost basic or *security rights*, by which he means the rights to physical security. This would include protection from murder, torture, rape or assault (1986, 445ff.).

On a lower level are nonbasic or *subsistence rights*, which denote a certain degree of economic security. Shue here includes ecological security, such as unpolluted air and water, as well as individual well-being, such as adequate food, clothing, shelter and minimal preventative health care. These rights are shared by the weakest elements in society, to which refugees generally belong.

Shue then introduces the concept of priority, which has some aspects of triage. The fulfilment of basic rights takes priority over all other activity, including the fulfilment of one's own nonbasic rights, while the fulfilment of nonbasic rights in turn takes priority over all other requirements. The order in which needs are to be fulfilled are therefore:

1. Basic rights
2. Nonbasic rights
3. All other needs and expectations.

Shue concludes that a refusal by the affluent to adhere to the concept of priority may hurt others physically (loss of security rights) as well as economically (loss of subsistence rights). Applied to refugees, refoulement would be seen as disregard by a nation of basic rights, while nonacceptance of refugees would affect their nonbasic rights. But, the latter act may be justified as an exercise of the nation's own basic right.

Garrett Hardin (1986) carries these ideas further in an article tellingly entitled "Life Boat Ethics: the Case Against Helping the Poor." He poses the questions: Does everyone on earth have an equal right to an equal share of its resources? What special responsibilities do rich nations have for helping the poor? If unlimited immigration to rich countries from poor countries is not possible, what will the result be? Extending the metaphor of the lifeboat, he calls us "adrift in an amoral sea." If the poor have needs and if all of the poor are our brothers we should, Hardin reasons, let them into our country to enjoy its benefits. But, he continues, if too many people already live in the country and more are admitted, does not everyone suffer? And if we only let in a few, how do we choose them?

Hardin solves the conundrum by demonstrating that the underlying premise is faulty. If all the rich nations help the poor and in the process become poor themselves, no one is helped in the end. If rich countries are to preserve some modicum of their ability to assist others, they must restrict the influx of those who might weaken the country. In turn, poor countries have to learn that they cannot be dependent on richer countries. If, instead, they were preparing for hard times, they could deal with its challenges.

Of course, one of the major problems of poor countries is overpopulation, and in this respect their governments must be held responsible. Richer countries should teach the poorer how to use their industrial and natural resources creatively, so that they could achieve true independence. We have to be harsh, says Hardin, in order to preserve ourselves. Applying Shue's principle of priorities, Hardin clearly comes down on the side of those who "have" and against those on who "have not." He would severely restrict the flow of refugees and immigrants.

The View from China [20]

Natural law and human rights were repeatedly treated in ancient Chinese philosophy, but there were distinct differences between the concepts arrived at by the Chinese and the natural law theories of European culture. While the West emphasized law and distinguished it from morality, Confucianism did not differentiate between morality and law.

The starting points of the two types of philosophy are similar: in both, natural law is understood to be obligatory for all human beings simply because they are human, and they are human because they are children of the Divine. In Chinese thought this is expressed by *Tian Tao*, "the way of Heaven."

The "rule of law" favoured by Western society stands in contrast to the Chinese concept of "society ruled by *Li*." *Li* is the central notion in Confucian theory. Literally it means rite, etiquette or gift—concepts that are clearly distinct from the ordinary meaning of law.

Li should be the main means of regulating relations between people. While the power of law relies on the means of enforcement, a *Li*-ruled society bases itself on tradition, ethics, morality, custom and public opinion—whose combined force may be as strong or even stronger than Western-style legal enforcement.

Li reflects the Chinese concept of an inner harmony that exists between human beings and nature, and thus the theory of natural law in ancient China was primarily related to ethical rules and moral regulations—that is, to *Li*.

With the rise of the Han Dynasty (from 206 B.C.E. on), Confucian precepts became a dominant factor in Chinese culture. Heaven was seen as the "colour" of rationality and morality. The way of punishment was to be by *Wang-Tao*: cultural education and instruction in morality, in other words, *Li*, the overarching way of unifying the human being with Heaven.

Zai Zhang[21] developed these precepts by stressing four major points:

1. The human being is part of nature.
2. Nature has its own general laws to which human beings have to submit.
3. Human nature is the heavenly way itself, for moral principle is consistent with natural law.
4. The ideal of life is to achieve the harmony between Heaven and the human being.

Traditional Chinese society did not see human rights as adhering to all human beings as such, but only to those of a certain social position. For example, the monarch was both the highest political ruler and also the owner of all property. In ancient China, people had the right to *use* property, but could not *own* it. The whole system of feudal centralization ran counter to the concepts of individual rights, freedom and democracy. It appears that the principle on which feudalism rested is reflected in modern China as well, so that the theories of Marxism and communism, which underlie its government, strike a traditional chord in much of Chinese society.[22]

Postscript: The Magna Carta as Natural Law

The Magna Carta—signed at Runnymede, England, on June 15, 1215— was not an innovative document but a codification of existing practices. It came at a time when writing was still the province of the few and was considered a guarantee of stability. The document enshrined the rights of the barons vis-à-vis the King and prevented the latter from overstepping his bounds. It was not directed at the rights and privileges of ordinary subjects—that was still in the future. Geoffrey Hindley has explained why we should not see the Magna Carta as concerned with human rights in the modern sense (1990, 179).

While the Magna Carta applied to "all the free men of the realm," protecting them from unlawful incursions by the King, this was not the same as the liberties that we have come to believe are the rights of all human beings.

A century and a half later, in 1354, the basis of application was broadened, and from then on the law held that no man "of what state or condition so ever shall be put out of his land or tenement or put to death without being brought to answer by due process of law."

The notion of natural law derives in part from an idea that found a home in England: every member of a community has certain natural rights. Commenting on this affinity, Hindley says:

> This idea of birth right arose essentially under the influence of the popular conception that certain rights confirmed in the Magna Carta as the special status rights of the barons were the habitual liberties of all Englishmen as such.[23]

Perhaps the greatest impact of the Magna Carta was felt not so much in England as in the New World, where the old charter was updated with new ideas. In the United States especially, freed from the restraints of English tradition, the principles of the Magna Carta were applied more broadly, and individual liberty became the undergirding of American civil law. The influence of the Puritans, moreover, superimposed upon the natural law of the Magna Carta the biblical emphasis on the divine origin of all rights. Thus, liberty came to be seen as having two main streams: one deriving from divine law and the other from natural law.

Even though human rights are recognized in the abstract, they need implementation in the world of national intercourse, for nations sign covenants and other agreements not to create these rights but to uphold and protect them.[24] However, another theory claims that rights exist only because of agreements to uphold them, that in fact no duties or obligations exist independent of agreements except the natural duty to honour one's agreements.[25] In this scenario, stateless persons would have no rights because they are not protected by any contractual agreement. Rights, then, would not be "natural" but merely an expression of a nation's contractual baggage.

This analysis points up a basic controversy about the nature of human rights. If they do not flow from religious, moral or "natural" (for instance, social or biological) sources, and the state is the repository and ultimate creator of such rights, individuals are at the mercy of the nation in which they happen to be located—either as citizens and/or resident aliens or as refugees. The state dispenses asylum, the refugee has no right to it; the state chooses to honour or dishonour this "obligation." If the state is the author and source of all rights, and refugees are not protected by a larger body from which to draw their legal strength, they are at the mercy of changing political circumstances.

This situation has prevailed for a good deal of the twentieth century and, despite occasional attempts at international intervention, has not been seriously threatened. The hesitation of the international community to intervene in the Bosnian crisis highlighted this moral failure.

In the retributive language of biblical morality, the conundrum can be stated as follows: we cannot ask for nor expect from God any treatment better than that which we ourselves accord to a stranger in our midst (Haim Cohen 1984, 166).

Hospitality

Roots

Early societies regarded the stranger as an enemy and the land outside the tribal borders as infested by demons. The magic powers of the stranger were feared because they were unknown. Still, strangers had to be dealt with because of commerce and migration.

In Greek myth, Zeus' surname was Xenios (from *xenos* meaning stranger or alien), which suggests that hospitality (from *hospes*, the Latin word for guest) was a divine command and its breach was considered a sin.[26]

In Iceland, folktales relate elaborate laws of hospitality, which allowed strangers to stay for extended periods of time. Later on this was narrowed to a stay of three days—an echo of basic distrust of the stranger, perhaps understandable in such an isolated locale.[27]

It might appear that hospitality has no moral foundation, but was an accommodation built on fear and thus functioned initially as a protective device. If morality were an operative element in it, hospitality would have to contain a viable dosage of altruism, which it does not always seem to have. Thus, hospitality could be seen foremost as an exercise in self-interest. (See further the discussion of African hospitality in Chapter 9 below.)

However, the Israelite tradition casts serious doubts on this construction. The Book of Exodus (22:20, 21) says: "You shall not wrong a stranger or oppress him, for you yourselves were strangers in the land of Egypt. You shall not ill-treat any widow or orphan." The position of the stranger, the widow and the orphan is significant, for they represent the weak in society, and they were placed under God's direct protection: "If you do mistreat them I will heed their outcry as soon as they cry out to Me" (22:22). The widow and orphan are protected in other Near East legislation as well, but the addition of the stranger is unique to the Hebrew Bible. All Israel had suffered the fate of strangers in Egypt, and thereafter "stranger, widow and orphan" together became the touchstone of biblical justice, and their protection was raised to a divinely supported principle, with God as its guarantor. God is the one to whom the weak may appeal and who will assist them in their plight, for the Divine nature is infused with love and concern for them.[28] The book of Sirach considers the sense of hospitality as a special gift of God.[29]

The stranger, or *ger*, is mentioned more than fifty times in the Torah, and the rest of the Bible further supports the need for treating him kindly. *Ger* was the term applied to the resident non-Israelite who could no longer count on the protection of his erstwhile tribe or society. This was not so with the *nochri* or *zar*, foreigners whose abode in Israel was temporary and who had not abandoned their own protective background. The *ger* was on his own and was to be given every consideration and care so that not only his rights but also his feelings were safeguarded. He must never be shamed, much like a debtor whose status is treated in the laws immediately following.

The Midrash used the text's caution about the stranger for an extensive exploration of the subject.[30] Again and again the Israelites were reminded that they themselves had been strangers in Egypt. Even as God had then heard the cry of the oppressed, so would He hear the cry of the weak at any time. Similarly, the Talmud says: "Hospitality [to humans] is greater even than receiving the Divine Presence."[31]

It is noteworthy that the tale of Sodom and Gomorrah (Genesis, Chapter 19) gave rise to similar considerations. The Rabbis speculated as to what the grievous sin of these two cities really had been. One of the answers provided was that the cities' streets were paved with gold and that, in the case of Sodom, the residents flooded the approaches so that strangers could not come to partake of their wealth (Plaut 1981, 82).

The Nature of Hospitality

It is generally recognized that our feelings regarding strangers are ambivalent, and probably weighted more towards the hostile side. Nouwen (1974, 3) suggests the reason:

> Someone who is unfamiliar, speaks another language, has another colour, wears a different type of clothes and lives a lifestyle different from ours, makes us afraid, and not seldom, hostile.[32]

While Nouwen claims that hospitality is itself a biblical term, this is in fact not so—though the practice of hospitality is demonstrated by a number of biblical figures, as exemplified by the story of the strangers who visited Abraham (Genesis, Chapter 18) and the repeated command to love strangers and treat them like the homeborn (e.g., Leviticus 24:22; Deuteronomy 10:19).[33]

Hospitality has been defined as

> primarily the creation of a space where the stranger can enter and become a friend instead of an enemy ... [i.e., the host forestalls hostility] strangers can enter and discover themselves as created free—free to sing their own songs, speak their own language, free to leave. (Nouwen 1974, 8)

He notes that North American parlance turned the biblical practice of hospitality into "soft, sweet kindness, tea parties, bland conversation, a general atmosphere of coziness." Instead, he sees hospitality as a divine potential of the host, a "hidden gift" that makes it possible for the guest to accept it with confidence. This runs counter to Western society, in which people are prevented from meeting each other and instead tends to make them into strangers to one another, each wearing a defensive armour that protects them from the other.

Amongst the Bedouin

A personal experience of Bedou hospitality in Arabia occasioned this observation:

> The Bedou is proud, touchy and independent. But above all, perhaps, he is hospitable, a characteristic remembered by van der Meulen (who travelled in Saudi Arabia between 1926 and 1972). I shall never forget the poor master of a primitive goat-hair tent, reacting to my polite greeting, "Peace upon you, oh master of this house of hair," by saying, "Foreigner, you are welcome, be my guest, Allah has given me plenty, there is also food for you." Then you sit down and eat a piece of hard, dry bread, some milk, and perhaps some rice. It is dirty and there is sand in it. But you eat, and praise the goodness of the unexpected meal, and you have made a friend for good.[34]

Postscript: Human Rights from Locke to Hitler

John Locke, in his *Letter on Toleration* (1689), argued that no church should have the government-supported power to restrict the religious observance of others and that no government should rule except with the consent of the governed. Locke relied on natural law as the basis for his argument.

> Men being ... by nature all free, equal, and independent, no one can be put out of this estate and subjected to the political power of another without his own consent, which is done by agreeing with other men, to join and unite into a community where they are comfortable, safe and peaceably living, one amongst another, may secure enjoyment of their properties, and greater security against any that are not of it. Any number of men may do, because he injures not the freedom of the rest; they are left as they were, in the liberty of the state of Nature.[35]

One hundred years later, Edmund Burke (1790) opposed parliamentary reform in Great Britain and was a staunch critic of the French Revolution.[36] His works became the staple reference for European conservatism. For him, rights were not derived from nature but from tradition, and thus any radical alteration in the status of the *ancien régime* was intolerable. He did not perceive himself to be the advocate of tyranny, but over a hundred years later he would often be referred to as an authority who would sustain a prohibition of change and accommodation.

In the New World, Thomas Paine (1791) attacked Burke's condemnation of the Declaration of the Rights of Man, the chief humanitarian product of the French Revolution, and ridiculed his assessment of the Declaration as "paltry and blurred sheets of paper about the rights of man." In Paine's view, natural rights were those which pertained to humans who, by dint of their being members of society, were entitled to security and protection.

A different chord was struck by the purveyors of modern fascism. In 1922, Benito Mussolini asserted that human beings do not exist as individuals but only as a collective, in that any rights given them come from the collective and not from any natural state that they may enjoy as persons on their own. To him, natural law urges people towards selfishness; it is the collective, the fascist state, which moulds them into a perfect community.

A few years later, in 1926, while interned in Landsberg prison, Adolf Hitler assigned human rights exclusively to the "Aryan race." To him, there was no law of nature which made all human beings equal; rather, the world was divided into the Aryan race and the others, all of which were inferior. He argued that, for the formation of higher cultures, the existence of inferior human types was one of the most essential preconditions, and that the first human culture was based less on the tamed animal than on the use of inferior human beings.

Notes

1. For instance, Exodus 23:9. See also Plaut (1981), 582. In Christian tradition, Jesus and his family became strangers in Egypt, thus reliving the experience of their people (Matthew 2:13–15).

2. Amos 9:7.

3. In various other versions (for instance, King James, New Standard Version, and New English Bible), the numbering is 23:15–16.

4. Tractate Gittin 45a.

5. Orthodox Jews and Christians take this rule to have been revealed by God to the Israelites at Mount Sinai (most likely in the thirteenth century B.C.E.), while biblical critics place the completion of the document at a much later date. But even so, since much of Torah (the Pentateuch, or Five

Books of Moses) is based on long oral traditions, there is good reason to suppose the high antiquity of the rule of nonrefoulement of slaves.

6. See Plaut (1981), 1249; Milgrom (1990), 504–9. The cities of refuge west of the Jordan were Hebron, Shechem and Kedesh; and east of the Jordan, Golam, Ramoth and Bezer. For an older treatment, see Bulmerinq (1853; reprint 1970).

7. For an example from the tenth century B.C.E., see I Kings 1:50; 2:28–30. Milgrom (1990, 508) suggests that Exodus 21:13–14 was the earliest stage of altar asylum. After Solomon built the First Temple, the institution of the asylum altar was abolished and replaced with the six asylum cities spread throughout the land.

8. Just how this transition from the Hebrew Bible to the Church was made is not clear; see Bulmerincq (1853; reprint 1970) p. 74.

9. Article 1179.

10. Sr. Leddy had previously recounted as a time of personal visitation her meeting of a person whose refugee claim had been rejected and who confronted her with the need to return home and face death.

11. This same missionary undertone is in fact also observable in the development of the Jewish concept of protection. In the Bible the term for stranger is *ger*, but in later usage it also includes the meaning "one who has been converted."

12. Redacted at the end of the second century.

13. *The Encyclopedia of Islam*, s.v. "dakhil."

14. Ibid., s.v. "djiwar." I am grateful to Dr. Liyahat Takim for his helpful comment.

15. Deuteronomy 33:27 and in many Psalms, e.g., 9:9, 46:1.

16. The chief works of those cited are: Aquinas, *Summa Theologica* (1266–73); Grotius, *On the Law of War and Peace* (1625); Hobbes, *The Leviathan* (1651); Locke, *Two Treaties on Government* (1690); Montesquieu, *Spirit of the Laws* (1748); and Rousseau, *Social Contract* (1762).

17. In earlier days, the Rabbis had already developed this concept when they postulated that God had implanted in all human beings a sense of social equity and had given them seven (so-called Noahide) basic laws they must observe. See Plaut (1981, 70–71); also Acts 15:20, 29.

18. Maritain, following Christian theology, assumes that when the Christian Gospels are fully understood, natural law will be seen in its perfection. For a survey of natural law, see *Die Religion in Geschichte und Gegenwart*, sub "Naturrecht," vol. IV (1960), 1360ff.

19. For a discussion, see Werhane, Gini and Ozar (1986).

20. Based on a research paper, prepared for this study by Jian Kang (1992, unpublished).

21. Sung Dynasty (960–1279 C.E.).
22. I have not been able to ascertain how these approaches impacted on refugee issues, if at all, since China has rarely functioned as an asylum nation.
23. Hindley (1990, 182) quoting Weber.
24. Nickel (1983, 34) calls this "Modest Contractarianism."
25. Nickel, ibid., calls this "Radical Contractarianism."
26. See Genesis 19:5; Judges 19:15 and following.
27. See also Julius Caesar, *De Bello Gallico*, XI:23; Tacitus, *Germania*, Chapter 21.
28. See Plaut (1981, 582).
29. Sirach 31:28.
30. The Midrash was a later body of biblical interpretation.
31. *Babylonian Talmud*, Shavuot 35b.
32. See the discussion of *hostis* in Chapter 6, under the subheading, "In-Groups and Out-Groups."
33. The term for hospitality, *hakhnasat orchim*, is post-biblical.
34. *The Illustrated Encyclopedia of Mankind*, 198.
35. Despite Locke's reference to nature, his attitude towards natural law was ambiguous and never treated systematically; see Horwitz (1990); others interpret him differently. It might be noted that for six years Locke felt it safer to live in Holland than at home.
36. Burke's chief work was *Reflections on the Revolution in France*.

4

A Look at History

Exiles and Refugees

Historically speaking, being condemned to exile antedated the conception of being a refugee. In fact, the story of humanity—as told in the Hebrew Bible (Genesis, Chapter 3)—begins with the exile of Adam and Eve from the Garden of Eden.

Greek mythology too is replete with stories of exile—such as the tale of Io who was expelled by Hera—and this mythology was reflected in Greek policy. Paul Tabori calls it "a means of preserving peace" and labels it, as a social institution, a Greek invention (1972, 46).[1]

In 471 B.C.E., Themistocles was banished from Athens and went to Persia where he was treated with respect and generosity. A generation before, Alcibiades had also taken refuge with a Persian ruler, Tissaphernes, after having been accused of being a ring leader in an attempt to overthrow democracy and the Athenian constitution.

Except for the death penalty, exile was the harshest punishment, and was either for a fixed period or permanent. The punishment was also used by the Romans (Tabori 1972, 62) and applied liberally by the medieval Christian Church to the Jews, who were expelled from various countries over many centuries.[2] At times, exile was presented to the accused as an alternative to other punishment and was made to appear as a voluntary choice. In any case, the result was that exiles were forcibly separated from their home.

The term exile is today applied more and more rarely; it usually represents a state of "self-exile" (often for cultural reasons). Or, as happened in the Soviet Union, it was occasionally initiated by the government (as in the case of Alexander Solzhenytsyn). While refugee is the preferred and almost exclusive term for the displaced person today, elements of the old use of exile still persist. For while a country may not wish to acknowledge it publicly, its government may have a policy of "encouraging" certain parts of the population to leave. An example is the displacement of Muslims by the Serbs in Bosnia; there the policy of exiling portions of the population has turned them into refugees. The term exile may thus be said to have retained a conceptual existence. Otherwise, exiles have all become refugees.

The phenomenon of refugees has existed since the beginning of recorded history, and doubtlessly preceded it. Tribal groups and larger units in all parts of the world have from time to time been on the move. Most often their need was to find new pastures or hunting grounds, new lands that would yield a more secure livelihood. Occasionally people fled wars or political oppression.

But whatever the reason, all of them had a common need: to leave their habitual place of residence and search out a new environment. While today the term refugee, in accordance with international conventions, refers primarily to individuals and has a sociopolitical meaning, such a construct tends to obliterate the most ancient and natural causes of population movements. Nature itself rather than social pressure was, and to this day remains, a major cause of displacement.

The enshrinement of asylum in law also has a long history. Around 1280 B.C.E., the Egyptians and Hittites agreed to a pact that provided for the extradition of refugees. It stipulated that people who fled from one jurisdiction to another had to be returned and would not be granted asylum. However, the treaty went on to say, in such cases the returned refugee would not be punished in his homeland.[3] We have no record to show how meticulously this provision was observed by either party, nor must we assume that we have here the origin of refugee legislation or the concept of nonrefoulement.

Fugitives and Strangers in Ancient China

In ancient days China knew a period of pacific intercourse, called *lieh kuo*, or the family of "coordinated states." They developed a system of customs that could be regarded as a kind of body of international law—though it was restricted to the area of China. As one historian described it:

> The clearest view of the public law which was acknowledged by this group of States, after they became independent, is undoubtedly to be sought for in their relations to each other while subject to a common suzerain ... The greater States were 12 in number and for ages their

distribution of territory was regarded as no less permanent than the order of the heavenly bodies. It was consecrated by the science of astronomy, as it then existed, and an ancient map of the heavens gives us a duodecimal division, where the stars of each portion are formally set apart to preside over the destinies of a corresponding portion of the empire. (Martin 1901, 432)

This arrangement also included a number of substates, which makes it somewhat comparable to the medieval Holy Roman Empire.

Independent states exchanged envoys, who, while generally deemed sacred, were at times arrested and even executed. This happened when they were considered spies, and the punishment was tantamount to a declaration of war.

A number of ancient treaties dealing with fugitives and strangers are extant. One, going back to 544 B.C.E., was concluded between the prince of Cheng and a coalition of princes who invaded his territories. One of the articles agreed to said that fugitives from justice would be surrendered.[4]

We do not know to what kind of fugitives this article refers. It may be assumed that, even though the treaty provided for it, such surrender did not always take place when political considerations demanded contrary action.

Strangers were, however, mentioned in an earlier compact, drawn up when the Imperial House still had greater control. This contract preceded the one noted above by about a hundred years. It stresses good morals, provides rules for social intercourse and aims at raising the character of the official hierarchy. One of the rules stipulates that one must not neglect strangers.

While the moral rules were thus stated, no details describe how they were carried out.

Greeks and Romans

It is generally agreed that the ancient Greeks, who developed the right of asylum considerably, derived it from religious sources. While early references to such rights spoke of them only with regard to certain classes or groups of persons, privileges were later extended to slaves as well.

Since Greece was increasingly divided into autonomous city-states, some of the principles of the Egyptian-Hittite treaties surfaced there as well. Through these intra-Grecian arrangements, the right of asylum underwent a subtle, yet fundamental change. The various Greek cities began to consider the right to asylum not as a subjective right of the person seeking refuge, but rather as a right of the city-state to grant it. On the one hand this development appeared to be progressive, since asylum was being considered as the concern of the community. On the other hand it was retrogressive in that it was now the city-state, rather than the individual, to whom this right was assigned.[5]

In Rome, where the supremacy of the state was no longer doubted, asylum—separated from its religious origins—became a dubious concept which, if exercised at all, was a right of the Roman Empire. Reciprocity with other states found no support, and Tacitus tellingly considers the example of Greek asylum as a nonsensical custom which encouraged the worst elements of a population to find protection "under the pretense of Divine tradition."[6]

Refugees in Modern Times

We have seen that the acceptance of forced or voluntary exiles by other nations could be classified as aspects of refugee acceptance. While examples can be drawn from regions as different as the Greek city-states and China, it seems that no recognizable and enduring patterns developed from these occurrences.[7] Such patterns are not observable until relatively recent times and, as Otto Kimminich properly notes, are traceable to religious intolerance.

> During the reign of Mary Tudor, 30,000 Englishmen fled to Holland; 20,000 Protestants had to leave Salzburg in 1732 and found refuge in East Prussia; the cancellation of the Edict of Nantes on November 16, 1685 was the signal for the flight of innumerable French Protestants who were given a friendly reception in England and on the continent.
>
> The ready reception of these religious refugees was of course related to the fact that they went to lands of asylum where their co-religionists were in power or at least possessed considerable influence. Their common religion created a solidarity beyond natural borders, thus removing the right to asylum—for the first time in many centuries—from the accidents of political rivalries and power constellations and created the foundation of common interests. (1968, 16–17)

Thus, religion and politics were intertwined, and the granting of asylum became a political matter, mirroring the persecution at home which was not merely religious but frequently political as well. In any case, we find here the foundations of the modern institution of asylum and note that—much like in ancient days (see the Hebrew Bible,

Numbers 35:6–34; Deuteronomy 23:16–17)—asylum had primarily a religious foundation.

But it was not long before religious motivations increasingly gave way to political considerations, as Kimminich points out:

> This [trend] showed itself clearly for the first time when in 1848 a wave of revolutions swept across Europe. In the next year Switzerland already accommodated 12,000 political refugees from Austria, Prussia and Russia. All three lands of origin requested the extradition of these refugees and even considered a declaration of war on Switzerland when the latter did not yield to the requests [8] ... After the repression of the Hungarian uprising of 1848 by the Habsburgs, many Hungarians fled to Turkey. Russia (which had a role in suppressing the uprising) and Austria requested the refugees' refoulement, and quoted certain old treaties which allegedly contained an obligation of Turkey to extradite the refugees ... The question began to interest European governments. Lord Palmerston sent a message to the English ambassador in St. Petersburg, on November 6, 1849, commenting that in principle no nation should return political refugees, except where there was a contractual obligation to do so. He based his opinion on the right of hospitality and the requirements of humanity as well as natural sentiments which rebel against such extradition. (1968, 17)

Turkey replied that its honour was at stake as well as the humanity of the Sultan, and since both France and the United States took the part of Turkey, Russia and Austria relented.

Until nearly the end of the nineteenth century, international borders remained wide open, apart from a few exceptions. For instance, the United States would require immigrants and or refugees to pass certain health tests, primarily relating to tuberculosis and eye diseases. Here and there some restrictions on undesirable refugees had been introduced but were later dropped. On the whole, refugee legislation was minimal, and the distinction between immigrants and refugees was largely theoretical. Refoulement was rare, if not altogether nonexistent.

In some areas, such as China and Japan, traditional restrictions regarding foreigners were still in effect. These restrictions were not instituted specifically against refugees, rather they reflected the desire of these nations to maintain as far as possible their cultural and human homogeneity, untainted by foreign additions.

As the nineteenth century wound down, new trends clearly emerged and in rather short order became the norm nearly everywhere, especially in Europe, whose major powers (which then included such smaller nations as Belgium and Holland) controlled much of the inhabited surface of the earth and had developed strong national identities. National borders now tended to become walls, and—as economic and political problems became more pronounced—this had severe consequences for poorer countries, where the pressure for new migratory outlets mounted considerably with the perfection of trans-Atlantic travel.

Mass movements became the order of the day. But it was not until World War I that nations generally began to buttress their identities with restrictive legislation. While heretofore political refugees consti-tuted a relatively small portion of human movement, they now became prominent. The structuring of new borders in Europe, the reapportion-ing of colonial empires and the establishment of communism in Russia created new conditions for displacement. The twentieth century may be characterized as a time when political aggression was met with closed borders and when (after World War II) refugee movements became worldwide.

Examples of this development were the trek of Jews from Russian-dominated lands and the flight of Armenians from Turkish oppression at the beginning of the century. Later on, the Middle East, Southeast Asia and much of Africa produced large-scale refugee populations. Refugee movements have become one of the dominant tragedies of our time. This development, which brings with it the whole question of *what* human beings owe to each other and *why* they do, has moved to the forefront of our considerations. Wandering people in the global village demand recognition.

Case History 1: The Huguenots

In the sixteenth century, Geneva became a centre of religious reforma-tion. The motivating force was a French-born theologian, John Calvin (1509–64), who made Geneva into what was called "a Protestant Rome, a citadel of the reform and an assured refuge against persecution."

For the citizens of Geneva the new reforming enthusiasm also had a political side: it asserted the city's independence and went so far as to exclude all Roman Catholics from its midst as a sign of its religious and political sovereignty.

Calvin was already dead when the French, at the opposite end of the religious spectrum, began to inveigh against the Protestants. In 1685, the king proclaimed that the Edict of Nantes, which had guaranteed the rights of nonconformists, was now abrogated. The Huguenots, which is what French Protestants were generally called, reacted by fleeing, their homes. The goal for many was Geneva, the French-speaking city where Protestants were welcomed.

Geneva had become a new biblical "city of refuge," and the Huguenot arrivals had become "refugees"—a term which thereafter gained increasing currency. Each of the newcomers, regardless of age or sex, was given half a crown for finances, and hospitals in Switzerland were ordered to prepare sheds to shelter those who would follow and to accommodate them in the best way possible. The arrivals were not asked to pray in the Reformed Churches of Geneva, but instead were free to worship in accordance with their own traditions.

Jacques Flourney recorded his observations when he saw the newcomers arrive in November and December 1685:

> Every day there continued to arrive a great many of these poor people, and their number already exceeded many thousands ... by the 15th of November 10,000 ... had already received assistance.[9]

According to Charles Weiss (1854), the reception of the refugees was remarkable for its generosity: collections were made; the former bishop's palace was transformed into a hospital for those who could not find shelter in the homes of citizens; large rations of bread and firewood were distributed every day and collection boxes were placed every Friday at the doors of the churches. A general assembly of the refugees was convoked at Lausanne in order to consider means of relief. Not surprisingly, German authorities who had accepted the Protestant religion and ethic were asked to help.

At the time, Geneva, despite all its independence, was also a part of federated Switzerland, which encountered political difficulties with France because of the little nation's generous treatment of people whom the French considered traitors. The Swiss assured Louis XIV that the refugees used Switzerland merely as a temporary asylum, and that they were only stopping off before going on to permanent residences in Germany.

However, Louis XIV demanded that the refugees be returned to him, since many if not most had left without his permission. The Swiss authorities tried to appease him, but never executed any order repatriating these refugees. Relations deteriorated and the French threatened the Swiss with war, but no armed conflict took place. In 1686, despite violent gestures by the French, the cities of Berne, Zurich, Basle, Schaffhausen and others declared that they were ready to risk all in the sacred interest of religion and that they would continue to shelter the Huguenots. By 1696, 6,104 male refugees alone lived in Berne, and various organizational measures were taken in all cities to care for the indigent newcomers. Nevertheless, most refugees who came to Geneva were denied citizenship—probably because the authorities feared that the French would retaliate for this "offence." The political situation eased when the Swiss began to urge the refugees to seek permanent asylum elsewhere, after which diplomatic relations between France and Switzerland resumed.

The Huguenots clearly had left France and were received in Switzerland for religious reasons. The ready reception of the Huguenots in other countries to which they fled—primarily Prussia, Holland, England, South Africa and America—was also for religious reasons, but not for them alone. Frequently it was generosity combined with enlightened self-interest, for the Huguenots had special skills. Thus the "Great Elector" of Prussia, King Frederick William, welcomed them because of their potential assistance in rebuilding his country after the devastation of the Thirty Years' War. It helped, of course, that the king's wife was the great-granddaughter of Gaspard II de Coligny, a leader of the Huguenots during the early Wars of Religion (1562–98) (Reaman 1963).

Frederick William issued the Edict of Potsdam to counteract the cancellation of the Edict of Nantes. His country would serve as an asylum for the newcomers and every assistance would be extended to them. They would be free from taxation, and homes would be built for them. Industrial and agricultural workers were given a special welcome, as were the sprinkling of noblemen who were skilled in advanced military tactics. Throughout the country Huguenots helped advance the textile industry and the printing trade.

The king's son, Frederick the Great, granted the Huguenots further privileges when he became king: freedom from taxation for ten years, land without interest, meadows for their cattle, the right to govern themselves religiously, the right to establish special industries, and freedom from taxes on imported silk.

The freedom to govern themselves religiously, which the Huguenots enjoyed in Prussia, was also noteworthy because the Huguenots were not Lutherans like their hosts, but members of the Reformed Church, which Calvin had helped to form.

In sum, the Huguenots represented a new element in the political, social and moral history of the Christian West. By background and sometimes by language they were strangers in their host countries, but it was their religious persecution that caused them to be received with open arms. This was the other side of the religious wars that had plagued Christian Europe from the sixteenth century on, and which had devastated its central lands by the middle of the seventeenth century.

Protestants had gained their independence from the Catholic church after a long struggle and were ready to extend the fruits of religious independence to those in search of it. The Huguenot migrations may therefore be considered an important example of the exercise of religious impulses in that people in flight found permanent asylum in other lands. It revived in practice the biblical injunction mentioned previously and became an important precedent in the treatment of modern refugees.

According to John Joseph Stoudt,

> ... [A]lmost two million Huguenots fled France. For the most part they did not establish large French speaking culture islands among other peoples, only here and there did a refugee congregation continue to worship in French. They did not form large and homogeneous groups like the Dutch in South Africa, the Germans in Eastern Pennsylvania, or even like the Roman Catholic French in Eastern Canada. Rather, the Huguenots chose to let themselves merge with the cultural and economic life of their newly adopted lands, accepting the ways and molds of their new homes with eagerness. (Reaman 1963, 9–10)

Stoudt suggests that a major reason for this readiness to assimilate was the Huguenots' original purpose for religious revolt: to launch a protest against a corrupt civilization.

> Rightly or wrongly the Huguenots were seeking to revive French life by putting moral fiber back into the French character. And when France exiled them their attentions were centered, not with the old culture, but with the new life that lay ahead. This made them entrepreneurs, adventurers and good material for colonization.

Case History 2: Jews and Armenians

During the first part of the twentieth century two groups became paridigmatic refugees, the Jews and the Armenians. They had one major characteristic in common: they were looked upon as outsiders, thus representing the quintessential stranger.

It was a bitter and strange irony that the Jewish people of biblical days, who, to comply with the demands of their religion, battled xenophobia on their own part (see Chapter 3), became its perpetual victims during the next two and a half millennia.

Christian Europe dubbed them "the wandering Jew" and treated them in accordance with what such otherness implied. They never became part of any society, even though some individuals rose to stations of importance, in accordance with their usefulness to the ruling powers—only to be disposed of when the moment seemed propitious. During the thirteenth and fourteenth centuries, both England and France expelled their Jews in a paroxysm of religious fervour and prejudice, and those who fled found refuge in other Christian communities. This sad and sorrowful tale was repeated time and again until it climaxed in the Holocaust.

Throughout many of these centuries the otherness of the Jews could never be forgotten. They were often confined to ghettos at night, and during the day (when they moved among gentiles) they were marked by special badges and characteristic dress. The so-called Jew's hat, a creation meant to look ludicrous, served the purpose well. Since they were outsiders, their expulsion was considered a normal and justifiable act of the sovereign.

It is a wonder that Jews always found some place where they could start rebuilding their lives, even though the new community was often very much like the one which they had been forced to leave. Only occasionally, as in the expulsion of the Jews from Christian Spain in 1492, did most of them flee to and settle in Muslim lands, where they were generally treated better.

If the sources of the Jewish refugee condition were the refugees' religious and cultural otherness, why did other Christian potentates receive them? Certainly not because Jews were accorded a basic right to be accepted and certainly not (with the exception of the Jewish migration from Spain) because the recipient authority was culturally or politically different from the one that had just expelled them.

No study I know of has examined this particular aspect of either Jewish history in particular or refugee history in general. Because the Jews were reputed to have commercial skills which might benefit the new host nation, was it self-interest on the part of the receiving state? No doubt this played a role, but in part only. Was it the occasional papal bull asserting the humanity of the Jews that influenced parts of the Christian constituency? Hardly, for there were other papal pronouncements that spoke of the Jews in opposing terms. Pending further study, I surmise that Jewish acceptance in other societies had two foundations. First, the modern nation-state with its controlled borders and exclusivist tendencies still lay in the future. Second, wanderers seemed to be a natural part of the human landscape; they arrived, stayed and often departed. As long as they were "other" and not allowed to integrate, they presented no political danger. They were simply there to be utilized, and could be discarded when they were of no further use. They had no right to permanent settlement and in a sense remained "refugees in orbit."

In this respect they were very different from the Huguenots. While no Jew had ever been accepted as a permanent resident, the Huguenots were French citizens. Their flight also represented a new phenomenon: having left their old habitat, they planned to make their new one their permanent home. To put it (with some inexactitude) in contemporary terms, they were refugees who changed their status and became immigrants on arrival in their new locales. It was a fate not vouchsafed to Jews to any realistic extent until their migration from Europe to North America. On arrival there, they shed their status of stranger and became settlers—a first for them. In intrasocial relationships in their new communities, they might continue to be considered different in some regards, but their otherness no longer kept them from claiming their right to be equal members of the state. They were refugees in transit and immigrants on arrival. Such a quick transformation is fundamentally different from what we see today.

While Jewish and Huguenot refugees were created primarily by religious prejudice, and only secondarily by political and economic considerations, the Armenian expulsions and killings simultaneously demonstrated religious and political dimensions. That the Armenians were mostly Christians and their host country, Ottoman Turkey, was overwhelmingly Muslim was the religious cause; politically, the Armenians had dreams of independence and strong cross-border ties with their Russian kin, who were later given the status of a separate state within the Soviet Union.

Between 1890 and 1919 about one million Armenians were in flight, and another one and a half million died. According to Turkish claims, this happened because of politically motivated uprisings; according to Armenian claims, because of outright genocidal, murderous activities efficiently carried out. Turkish apologists also point out that Armenians in Turkey had a fair degree of autonomy, and a national assembly. Still, the overwhelming judgement of historians is that the Ottoman Turks engaged in genocidal excess at the beginning of the twentieth century (Kimminich 1968, 19)—a judgement that was popularized during the 1930s by the Austrian novelist Franz Werfel, in his widely read *The Forty Days of Musa Dagh*.[10] Kimminich estimates that while the exact number of refugees is no longer obtainable, about 400,000 fled to Russian Armenia, and another 460,000 to Europe and parts of the Near East.

In sum, from antiquity until recently, the reception of refugees had its roots primarily in religious convictions. God, or the gods, protected those who came to seek protection in sacred places, where human justice (or injustice) could not reach them. The Israelites and Greeks are the earliest exemplars and the medieval Christian Church adopted the idea of the church as sanctuary. The Romans, however, who bore no allegiance to such religious concepts, were not inclined to grant asylum in general. The earlier arrangement between the Egyptians and the Hittites, on the other hand, was purely a matter of national interests— although the expression in the document, that deliverance of refugees was not "right," leaves open the possibility or even likelihood that here too we are face to face with basically religious conceptions.

We thus see a dual development: refugees attained their unhappy status because of their religion, and when accepted elsewhere would frequently (though not always) find the accepting nation to be of their own religious persuasion. A latter-day example is Israel's Law of Return, which provides that every Jew has a right to settle in the land.[11]

As this study was being prepared, new religioethnic refugee movements were exploding in the former Yugoslavia. Bosnia's Muslim population was being forcibly ejected by Catholic Croats and Greek-Orthodox Serbians. In consequence of the ensuing war, Muslim Bosnians fled to various parts of Europe, with Germany accepting the largest numbers.

Case History 3: Strangers in the Realm of Islam—A Historical Retrospective

Essential to understanding Islamic attitudes towards refugees is the concept of *dhimma*, as developed by the *Shari'ah* (the canonical law of Islam), which regulates the rights of non-Muslims rather precisely. A distinction therefore exists between refugees who are Muslims and those who are not. If the refugees are Muslims, the obligation to receive them is clearly based on the concept of religious brotherhood. If they are not, other considerations come into play.

Until recently, Muslim refugees tended to flee to Muslim nations or countries where Muslims had a commanding majority. Their accept-ance there was a given and flowed from religious considerations, though their treatment varied with respect to the receiving country's particular economic, political and social circumstances.

But while the flight of Muslims to non-Muslim lands has become significant only in modern times, non-Muslim refugees who went to Islamic countries were a significant feature in history. The treatment of these "others," once they were incorporated into the nation or empire, was regulated by *dhimma*. Such persons came to be known as *ahl al-dhimma*, persons of contract or obligation. Both parties had obligations towards each other, though in the Muslim/non-Muslim relationships the right to draw the terms of obligation was the right of the dominant party—the Muslim community to which the stranger came.[12]

Dhimmi (non-Muslim residents) were created most frequently through military conquest. Here law and tradition made a difference between heathens on the one hand (who had few rights) and "people of the book" on the other. It is only the latter to whom the law of *dhimma* originally pertained. People of the book (*ahl al-kitab*) were Jews, Chris-tians and "Sabians" (probably Zoroastrians). Only they were accorded a particular civil status. In turn, they had to pay certain head taxes and, where applicable, realty taxes.

Despite the latitude granted to them, it was always understood that all their rights derived from the Islamic community and that their real property never ceased belonging to the host nation.

Jurisprudence arising from the Quran provided that the *dhimmi* were also obligated to distinguish themselves from the believers by their dress. They were not permitted to ride a horse or wear arms and had to pay respect to Muslims in general. Furthermore, *dhimmi* did not have full rights before courts in criminal law or with regard to marriage.

These restrictions were applied more or less stringently in various Islamic jurisdictions. However, when comparisons are made with Christian rule, non-Muslims were on the whole well-treated and their right to exercise their own religion not basically impaired. In return, *dhimmi* were expected to lead a modest and unostentatious life, in keeping with the fact that they did not enjoy full citizenship. Most important, especially in medieval times, was the right of non-Muslim communities to conduct their religious and communal affairs in a semi-autonomous fashion.[13]

Few attempts have been made to understand why the Ottoman Empire accepted the stream of Jewish refugees it did during the late Middle Ages. Salo Baron, in the multi-volume *Social and Religious History of the Jews*, though, did attempt to give some answers.[14] Characteristically, however, they contain no reference to underlying religious or ethical motivations but concentrate rather on the more accessible and common-place reasons that can be found in the realm of social, economic and political circumstances.

The Jewish position in Europe had reached a low point in the fourteenth and fifteenth centuries, with the expulsion of Jews from France (1306, 1393) and Iberia (1492, 1496–97), as well as from other parts of the continent. According to Baron, the sultans of the Ottoman Empire realized that they could benefit from the Jewish arrivals because they were economically and culturally advanced. There was also a negative reason: the Ottomans felt that since the Jews had been persecuted by the Christians, they would be intensely loyal to their new host.

But it was perhaps mostly the generous attitude of the Muslims that caused the Jews to become loyal and appreciative subjects. They had the freedom to travel and to participate in industry and commerce; they brought their medical and governmental experience to bear on their communities and, at the same time, because they were granted considerable autonomy, felt thoroughly at home.

The religious element surfaces in the granting of autonomous communal government not only to the Jews but also to other nationalities in the empire. This concession was based on ethnoreligious lines, not on territorial boundaries. The Quran recognizes the religious experience of Judaism and Christianity, and therefore minorities professing these faiths were not disturbed in their exercise of them and were also given the opportunity to continue their specific cultural expressions. In fact, towards the middle of the fifteenth century, Sultan Mehmed asked the religious minorities to appoint leaders who would represent them before the government—a mutually beneficial arrangement, because it increased the level of autonomy of the various minorities on the one hand, and gave the Ottomans greater opportunity for control on the other.

There was, however, an important distinction between the Jewish and Christian minorities: the latter had ties to important and powerful

European states to whom Islam was anathema; thus, Christians in the Ottoman Empire were suspected of what nowadays would be called dual loyalty. Because the Jews had no state of their own, their loyalty was considered more reliable.

In addition to these religious aspects, economic considerations also affected the refugees. Subsequent to the arrival of hundreds of thousands of Jews from Spain and Portugal in the 1490s, Sultan Bayezid II was moved to prohibit Jewish emigration from his lands because that would create a significant loss both to the economy and the treasury of the Sultan. To be sure, edicts like these were at variance with *Shari'ah*, but the history of the Ottoman Empire shows a departure from strict Islamic law whenever *realpolitik* required it (Baron 1983, pp. 6–44).

The enormous expansion of the Ottoman Empire during the sixteenth century, sometimes described as Turkey's Golden Age, is connected primarily with Sultan Selim I, Suleiman and Selim II. Sunni Muslims were in the majority and generally tolerant towards Jews, who experienced their own golden age in this century. The Jewish population in the empire increased, and this induced a voluntary migration of European and other Jews to the Ottoman Empire. Constantinople had 30,000 Jews, making that city home to the largest Jewish community in the early modern world. Other significant communities existed in Damascus, Aleppo, Jerusalem, Alexandria and Cairo.

Baron attempted to discover how the resident Muslims reacted to the new Jewish arrivals, but found little data. Some of these, though, were "negative." For instance, there were no complaints to the central government against the newcomers. Also, the cost of living appears to have risen, but only slightly, so that the immigrants were not blamed for a nonexistent problem.

However, problems did arise in 1553 from another side: the Christian minority. An Armenian group accused Jews of killing a Christian, and a Jew was killed in retaliation while others were arrested. Sultan Suleiman acted quickly and ordered that in the future all blood accusations had to be brought to the central government and could not be left to the control of the local authorities. Subsequent Sultans abided by this measure (Baron, 71ff).

This incident demonstrates the essential instability of minorities living in the empire. Jews, Christians and other non-Muslims could not be integrated into the mainstream of society and therefore remained outsiders—well-treated and often quite prosperous, but ultimately at the mercy of the ruler.

> The rapidity of the empire's growth and the ensuing enforcement by
> the authorities of a somewhat superficial, rather than an integral, unity
> in part masked its inherent weaknesses which, under changed na-
> tional and international circumstances, came strongly to the fore. It is
> not amazing therefore, that this Golden Age gave way to an era of
> turbulence and incipient disintegration. The Jewish communities, too,
> could not remain unscathed. (Baron, 121)

Thus, when the empire was threatened, the otherness of the
unintegrated minorities made them the prime victims of political and
economic instability.

A detailed study by Aryeh Shmuelevitz (1984) confirmed much of
Baron's research. The Jewish community was incorporated into the
empire as a *religious* group and, under the autonomous administration
system (*millet*), as an *urban* group. Since the *Shari'ah* did not deal
specifically with non-Muslims as a community, the *dhimma* system
became in time the vehicle for the treatment of new arrivals. It thus
confirmed that the refugees were—upon arrival—accorded the status
of *dhimmi*, which in principle was a concept clearly derived from
religious sources (Shmuelevitz, 15). Reflecting on this principle now,
one may fairly conclude that the motivations underlying acceptance of
the refugees were at least in part religious.

One finds, however, certain exceptions to the generally generous and
tolerant attitude exhibited by the Ottomans. There was, for instance, a
forced resettlement of Jews from smaller towns in Anatolia and in the
Balkans to Istanbul under Mehmet II. In addition, some forced conver-
sions of Jews to Islam took place, especially during the time of Bayezat
II, who not only forbade these converts to return to Judaism but also
closed some of the synagogues. Yet it was this same sultan who
welcomed the exiled Jews from Spain and Portugal. Shmuelevitz
therefore suggests that the likely reason for the acceptance of the Iberian
exiles was economic and not religiously motivated benevolence
(Shmuelevitz, 3).

This confluence of generosity towards arriving refugees on the one
hand and the restrictions imposed on them after arrival merely points
out that we may not speak of a single or even predominant motivation.
Clearly, political and social policies were important, and often dominant, factors. But on the other hand, the religious aspects of the *dhimma*
system were always in evidence. Islamic treatment of refugees during
the end of the Middle Ages and up to modern times may therefore be
said to rest at least in part on ethics derived from religious tradition.

In modern secular states with a Muslim majority, the old categories have lost much of their force, but with the increase of Islamic state supported fundamentalism, former distinctions have reappeared.

Notes

1. Note that the above-cited biblical institution of the "cities of refuge" provided for de facto exile, and Amos 1:15 (eighth century B.C.E.) spoke of God as sending the leaders of Ammon into exile (*golah*). Israel's leadership class itself was exiled in 586 B.C.E.

2. Augustus exiled the poet Ovid for reasons no longer known, and Tiberius banished four thousand persons to Sardinia for their "Egyptian or Jewish superstitions."

3. See Pritchard (1955), 200–3. Excerpts from the treaty will be found in Appendix A of this study.

4. Martin 1901, 440–41. See also R. S. Britton (1935).

5. See Kimminich (1968), 33. Bulmerincq (1970), 29ff., gives extended examples.

6. *Annals* III, 60ff.

7. Chinese examples, dating from the eighth century B.C.E., are recorded by Britton (1935), 616ff. These instances deal primarily with members of the nobility and of the royal households.

8. Kimminich, following Paul Bastid (1948).

9. Cited by Weiss (1854), 161–62.

10. For historical analysis, see for instance A. Mandelstam, *Das armenische Problem in Lichte des Völker-und-Menschenrechts* (1931); about the earlier massacres, see Johannes Elpsius, *Armenien und Europa* (1896). Similar to the Armenian refugee developments were those of another Ottoman group, the Assyrians. They lived in a small enclave and in 1915 declared their independence from Turkey.

11. See Chapter 8.

12. *Handwörterbuch des Islam* (1976), s.v. "dhimma."

13. Ibid.

14. Baron (1983), v. 18, passim.

5

Some Ethical Questions

Ethical Dimensions of Refugee Law

Ethics, said C. S. Milligan (1989), has to do with the means and ends as they relate to the values of life for the individual and society. Ethics is frequently contrasted with pragmatism: the former is supposed to be ideal and the latter, real. But perhaps it is the other way around. Perhaps policies which are merely pragmatic will in the end fail if they ignore the moral dimension.

To be sure, every code of ethics holds out ideals, and these have practical goals. The ethical impulse includes the interest of others in the perception of self-interest. Such inclusion is generally accepted when it comes to family relations or even the national interest (especially in times of crisis), but there is great reluctance to extend "practical ethics" to the global sphere. We feel that we owe people something in direct relation to their proximity to us.

The ethicist cannot overlook this innate human reaction—see the discussion of sociobiology in Chapter 6 of this study. We do take care of "our own" first, but how far the circle of legitimate self-interest goes and how much it is influenced by moral considerations is a question that is hard to answer in the abstract. Pragmatists frequently posture as moralists by pronouncing themselves as followers of an ideology. But ideologues will see theories first, while ethicists see human beings first and theories as necessary but secondary. Theories, moreover, can be changed if need be, according to the ethicist (Milligan, 168).

In the refugee area, Milligan establishes three principles that combine ethics and political realities:

1. A nation has the right as well as the need to regulate immigration. For it has to deal with limited resources,

employment problems, and the ability of newcomers to make social adjustments.

2. Politicians and administrations make administrative decisions and will bring their own moral principles to bear on their judgement.

3. People become refugees for a variety of reasons—they may fear death or other harm, persecution or starvation—but citizens of the potential host country often feel that merely wanting to improve one's life is not enough reason to apply for refugee status.

When refugee policy is discussed within the jurisdiction of a particular country, advocates of a more liberal admission of refugees will likely cite moral grounds as their reason, while those who argue for greater restrictions will give economic reasons for their position. But it is not always that clear-cut. Often—and especially in recent years—ethnic and religious reasons will play their role in the demand for more tightly closed borders. One need only think of the Bosnian/Serbian/Croat confrontation, the controversies in France and the riots in Germany.

Peter and Renata Singer (1988, 112ff.) have attempted to see these problems from a wider perspective. Richer countries, they say, will not want refugees from poorer countries. They will claim that refugees put a strain on their countries' resources and cause social unrest, and that newcomers do not have a right to demand what older residents have created for their own consumption. They will therefore either advocate the closing of borders altogether or, more usually, permit some refugees to enter but not enough of them to alter the quality of economic, social and cultural life of the host country. Thus, say the authors, the questions regarding a country's refugee policy can always be described in these terms: Do we let in all of the refugees? Do we let in some of the refugees? Do we let none in?

Providing permanent or temporary shelter is the first task for a country that offers asylum. Refugees are usually sheltered in poverty-stricken lands like Africa, which accommodates millions of refugees, or Pakistan, which has taken on much of the Afghan refugee burden. Remarkably, the poorer countries will make few distinctions between refugees who fit the narrow UN definition and those who come because of other, primarily economic and social, needs.

One must ask, do such people not have a right to better their lives? And who are those who will deny them that chance? Here, too, richer countries set a poor example. They are hesitant to share, while those who have little are more generous. It is precisely in the matter of refugee accommodation that this moral contradiction becomes most visible.

Morality and Self-Interest

The relationship between morality and self-interest in treating refugees has been explored by Howard Adelman. He identifies the role that bureaucracies and elite leadership groups play in forming the policy of most sovereign nations.

> The right of the authorities to accept or reject refugees is not simply a natural act of a state constituted to serve and enhance the self-interest of its members, but is a way of giving witness, of demonstrating the principles of such a state (as opposed, for example, to states ostensibly dedicated to the welfare of the citizenry as a whole). Countries founded to serve and enhance the "individual" self-interest of their members act differently than states constituted to serve the "collective" self-interest (as defined by a small core within their leadership). It is not surprising, for example, that in countries with a democratic liberal tradition (in contrast to Marxist-Leninist states) refugees are granted the right to claim status. Opening its doors to the claims of individual refugees exemplifies, in the best way possible, that the state exists to serve individual self-interested claims and not abstract principles of justice articulated by an elite ... The granting of rights to individual refugee claimants, therefore, is a logical extension and existential expression of a subjective set of beliefs, but it is also an objective standard by which the degree to which a state truly adheres to such principles can be assessed and judged. (Adelman, 1993)

Adelman further points out that the maintenance of international order is in the interest of all states, and that exploding refugee populations threaten this order. When nations that are capable of receiving refugees do not act, they will in effect force stateless masses to take explosive measures to demonstrate the hazards of their statelessness.

He effectively counters the oft-heard argument that when refugees are selected abroad their admission is more cost-effective than the expensive process of refugee determination that takes place inside a host country. He calls the former group "state-selected" and the latter "self-selected." State-selection can never take the place of self-selection, for the former is an administrative process, while refugee determination inside a nation is judicial in nature. *Cost-effectiveness can, morally speaking, never be the ultimate determinant in the balance between bureaucratic decision making and judicial determination.* Adelman, with tongue in cheek, therefore asks rhetorically whether it is not true that a judge is more cost-effective than a jury.

In this respect, self-selected refugees are "expensive," but they represent a very special group: they are either the ones in greatest need, which is why they have taken flight, and/or they are the ones with the most initiative and daring and will therefore likely be valuable additions to their host nation. In the long run, their cultural and economic contributions will more than repay the "expense" of their acceptance.

Positivists argue that morality is an aspect of biological self-interest. Undoubtedly there is a relation between them, and even in a distinctly nonbiological field like refugee acceptance, the intermingling of morality and national self-interest is apparent. Compassion and conviction, though, are also contributory determinants in shaping the fate of a nation.

A contemporary footnote may be added to these theoretical considerations. In 1992–93 U.S. military personnel was involved in relief operations in Somalia. After the initial enthusiasm that greeted the arrival of the American troops, the relief effort quickly ran into existing internecine warfare and yesterday's heroes were being called intruders.

Similarly in Bosnia, hesitant relief efforts could not be separated from political and military confrontation and, as has so often happened before and elsewhere, the motives of the United States were questioned. Was it a purely moral imperative that propelled them to institute humanitarian activities that cost hundreds of millions of dollars, or was it also an exercise in self-perceived world leadership?

To the unbiased observer it seems clear that the American people who supported both of the relief incursions and who knew that it was their tax dollars that financed them, did not mingle their own charitable inclinations with such political considerations. They felt overwhelmingly that, with adults and children starving and dying by the thousands, they—the citizens of the world's richest nation—had to do something and could not turn away, pretending that this was none of their business.

Did their government also want to do that which was politically advantageous when it responded to the humanitarian impulse of the voters? Probably. But, if so, does a government's self-interest not represent one side of the coin and the morality of the nation as a whole, the other? Again, the answer must be yes. Morality does not exist in the abstract, neither in the individual nor in a whole people. Yet it would be a perversion of history to claim that American self-interest was the motive in what was essentially a response to a humane impulse.

The Morals of Refugee Protection

James C. Hathaway (1991) notes that refugee protection, with all its avowed high purposes, does itself have serious moral flaws. Tracing the history of the UN Convention, he shows that its first version, passed in 1951, was primarily a reaction to European political developments before and after World War II. Before then, most major refugee movements flowed from Europe to other parts of the world, primarily the Americas, but the developments of the 1930s and 1940s created intra-European refugee migrations. The Convention finally arrived at in 1951 speaks of refugees who had suffered dislocation in Europe before that year. The original version thus was "eurocentric," and only the Protocol of 1967 made it applicable everywhere and without time limitations.[1]

While the Soviet Union wanted a different approach, the Western nations prevailed in stressing the search for individual liberty as the central feature of refugee protection—a view rejected by the communists at the time. As Hathaway explains, "Fear of persecution was such an open-ended term that the West was able to manipulate it and thereby able to continue giving ideological dissidents, especially anti-Communists, international protection" (1991, 7).

The UN Convention thus emphasized the Western point of view in that it stressed political rights, race, religious freedom, or the right to belong to a certain social group or—most important—to hold political opinions that were at variance with those of the ruling government. Communist countries and, before them, fascist states, considered the inclusion of such definitions as methods of interfering with their internal politics. From their perspective what was needed included protection for people who had suffered violations of socio-economic rights, among them health care, education and shelter and food. These, however, were not protected under the Convention. By excluding them, Hathaway says, the Convention "adopted an incomplete and politically partisan human rights rationale" (1991, 8).

The original Convention was also deficient in that it addressed only pre-1951 events in Europe and not the problems of the developing world, though they were already then in view and growing. While in 1967 the United Nations did adopt a Protocol that expanded the Convention definition to include refugees from everywhere and not just from or in Europe, this change did not alter the substance of the refugee definition. It still excluded Third World refugees, most of whom were fleeing from natural disasters, wars and economic or all-encompassing political upheavals, rather than fleeing from persecution.

In the present formulation of the Convention *cum* Protocol, "persecution" is construed narrowly, so that it overlooks the reality that wars and natural disasters frequently mask political persecution. And, in any case, it does not address the basic purpose of refugee protection: the alleviation of human suffering. Starving people trying to migrate to more promising pastures had throughout the centuries been considered legitimate refugees (although that terminology did not yet exist), but not today. Technically speaking, in all Western countries, people fleeing from social, economic and environmental distress are not now considered refugees.

While the UNHCR has broadened its care for refugees suffering from forced migration, the Convention lags behind such practices and realities. It appears that human suffering is not its primary motivation for assisting refugees. The interests of the potential host nation are considered superior to other claims. The only obligations a country has today under the terms of the Convention is to practise nonrefoulement. Nations, moreover, will insist that their greatest moral obligation is protecting the welfare of their own citizens. "We cannot help the whole world," say those who support this view, "we will help as much as we can, but we draw a line when helping others affects the well-being of our own people."

While it would be an exaggeration to claim that international refugee protection is bereft of basic moral considerations, they usually take second place. Killing may be prohibited under ordinary circumstances, but justified in cases of self-protection—individual or national. No nation can open its doors to all the world (even if all the world were to wish to take advantage of the possibility), and consequently the application of moral imperatives will be limited by some measure of self-interest on the one hand and arbitrary decisions (such as triage) on the other. Religious or philosophical ideals usually conflict with other requirements: one does not pursue them in a vacuum.

In this sense, morality and the sources from which its precepts and injunctions arise may be seen to urge individuals and nations to pursue certain goals and thereby to temper the excesses of self-interest. They always remind us that what we are doing to help people in need is less than what we could and should do.

Henry Shue (1989) has tried to explain the moral roots of this obligation. He believes it stems from the general human duty not to deprive others of their natural needs; to protect them from deprivation; and to aid those who in fact have been deprived.

Similarly, John Rawls sees in nonrefoulement an example of the exercise of natural duties

> ... of helping another when he is in need or jeopardy, provided that one can do so without excessive risk or loss to oneself ... Such duties hold between persons irrespective of their institutional relationships; they obtain between all as equal, moral persons ... they are owed not only to definite individuals, say to those operating together in a particular social arrangement, but to persons generally. (quoted in Goodwin-Gill 1988, 110)

To be practical, both Rawls and Shue agree that a certain degree of risk to oneself or one's community implicitly limits the duty to others. But just where self-interest ceases and moral obligation takes over can hardly be determined in theory alone.

Guy S. Goodwin-Gill (1988, 115) confronts these principles by emphasizing the need for burden sharing. To reject refugees is the negative side of our humanitarian impulses, while their accommodation is the measure of international or national morality.

H. Patrick Glenn (1992) has discussed a variety of safeguards in place in many nations that give these obligations legal expression. Chief amongst them is constitutional protection. Thus, Germany's constitution posited the absolute right of people to seek asylum within its borders, a policy which in 1992 led to severe internal disturbances and was subsequently amended (see Chapter 10). But though in other countries the constitution itself may not guarantee the right to asylum in such a broad manner, individual rights safeguarded by a constitution may in effect have a similar impact.

In Canada, the Supreme Court in the Singh decision (1985) accorded to any person inside the borders of the country—however briefly or possibly illegally—the right to due process. Once in Canada they are protected in their civil rights like everyone else. The biblical command comes to mind: "The stranger shall be to you like the home born."[2]

Us and Them

Fiji, a multi-island independent member of the British Commonwealth, is one of the newer nations in the world but may serve to illustrate an old, pervasive problem: the relationship between residents and immigrants/refugees.[3]

Long under colonial rule by the British, Fiji experienced a large influx of labour from India. In time these workers became the dominant economic force on the islands. As long as the British ruled, tensions between the native Fijians and immigrant Indians were at a low point, but, with independence, they began to grow and eventually broke out into the open. In addition to cultural differences, there were also religious divisions: the Fijians had been converted to Christianity while the Indians were and remained mostly Hindus.

Even though the latter have now been in the country for generations, native Fijians feel that their own culture has been suppressed or, at best, seriously adulterated by their presence. Parties have been founded along national lines and, consequent to a win by the native Fijians, a constitution has been fashioned that makes it difficult for the Indian segment to gain full citizenship. Thus, a difference has been introduced between "us and them," and the native Fijians claim that they are entitled to protect their cultural heritage against the newcomers. This distinction invites comparisons with other past and present nations. Says Joseph Carens:

> Think of cases where a state has excluded from citizenship people born and raised in the community. Nazi Germany did it under the Nuremberg Laws. South Africa did it under apartheid ... Their policies of exclusion from citizenship on the basis of race, religion, and ethnicity were centrally connected to what we find most morally abhorrent about those regimes.
>
> Of course, many contemporary states have citizenship laws that do not grant citizenship to everyone born and raised within its borders, and these policies do not arouse the same intuitive moral outrage as the policies of Nazi Germany and South Africa under apartheid. But that is largely because the implications of the formal citizenship policies are muted by other policies and practices, that acknowledge de facto many of the moral claims of those born and raised within a state, especially their right to stay and to be treated with respect and dignity. (1992, 24)

Here, the problems of present-day Germany come to mind: the denial of citizenship to most of its six million guest workers, some of whom have been in the country for forty years and have brought up children and grandchildren there. The spate of outrageous murders and incessant attacks on them as unwanted foreigners (especially the Turkish element) cannot be separated from their lack of full civil rights.[4]

Lately, the German government has planned a loosening of its rigid citizenship policies—trying to moderate somewhat the new constitutional amendment, which makes it virtually impossible for refugees to claim asylum. The proposed change in citizenship procedure was generally seen as a moral pay-off to still the opposition to the amendment.[5]

Yet, asks Carens, are not the claims of those who want to protect the historical culture of their own nation justified? Do they have no right of protection in the face of an overwhelming influx of immigrants and refugees?

> The requirements of justice set moral limits to the pursuit of cultural preservation as a goal. One obvious challenge to this line of argument is to ask the question, "Whose justice"?[6] This raises the issue of the relation between respect for cultural difference (an ideal implicit in the goal of the preservation of minority cultures) and moral relativism. If different cultures embody different moral views, at least to some extent, isn't it a form of cultural imperialism to use the standards of one culture to judge another?
>
> I do not think that this challenge can be dismissed out of hand. There is a real danger that in making judgments about other societies we will be led astray by misunderstandings or misinterpretations of practices and institutions different from our own. Anyone who has encountered the smug (and in important respects, unfounded) sense of moral superiority of even the best of 19th century British liberals like John Stuart Mill, ought to feel some trepidation that his or her late 20th century judgments will be seen by later generations as similarly tainted. (Carens, 1992)

Both politicians and moralists have to make some choices in this regard, choices that are not necessarily the same for all cultures, nations and times. The ideas of multiculturalism, of which Canada has been a prime proponent and practitioner, are rejected in many if not most countries and face significant opposition in Canada itself.

All of this affects refugees and their claim to asylum. Present-day Germany has closed its borders in part because of the sharp economic downturn it has experienced with the rise of unemployment and dislocation, but in part also because of xenophobia, which has been made worse by violence.

The fears of the native-born that their culture will be undermined is usually unjustified. In the long run, immigrants of all kinds tend to assimilate by accustoming themselves to and accepting the prevalent mores and traditions, and rarely change the character of their new home. Such fears can be turned to advantage if the contributions of the newcomers are seen as an enrichment of the resident culture.

On the other hand, it cannot be denied that countries of immigration, such as Canada and the United States, have been profoundly affected by immigration. In my view, this has caused not only enormous diversification of cultural modes but an enlargement and growth of both nations. Inbreeding usually leads to narrowness and rigidity, while the open acceptance of other traditions enlarges the perimeters of one's own civilization.

Therefore, rather than reproduce a straightjacketed set of rules, it would be better to proceed with a sense of both openness and compromise—compromise that must be made by the resident community *and* the newcomers. Each must accept the other and both will gain in the process.

Asylum for Terrorists—A Moral Dilemma

During the 1970s and 1980s, the question of whether suspected or convicted terrorists should be granted asylum in another country was extensively debated. Atle Grahl-Madsen (1985, 46ff.) points out that for 150 years extradition treaties featured a clause that contracting states had no obligation to extradite political offenders, and the 1957 European Convention on Extradition has been understood to prohibit extradition of such offenders.

But, with the spread of international terrorism, the traditional prohibition on extradition has been questioned. Certain acts like war crimes, hijacking or kidnapping were deemed by some as unacceptable regardless of motive, and there was widespread feeling that those who had committed such acts should not be able to avoid extradition and punishment merely by claiming that their crimes had a political basis.

According to Grahl-Madsen, the many conventions concerning aspects of terrorism adopted during the last decade have been based on the principle *aut devere, aut punire,* which means the state in whose territory the culprit is found should either extradite or prosecute and punish him/her.

To this end a number of international treaties were put in force, among them the Hague Convention for the Suppression of Unlawful Seizure of Aircraft (1970), the Montreal Convention (for similar crimes, 1971), and the European Convention on the Suppression of Terrorism (1977).[7]

Not all crimes are covered by these conventions, and it has therefore been suggested that there should be two levels of consideration. One would address the most serious acts, generally labelled "crimes against humanity," while others such as killing a political enemy in a third state that has no part in the conflict, could be considered a political offence.

Whether or not to extradite the perpetrator raises yet another, and in some ways, more fundamental problem, namely, whether extradition itself (whether pursuant to a treaty or otherwise) does not offend against the rule of nonrefoulement. What is at stake here, as in the question of asylum for terrorists, is the balance of two needs: the principle of protection and the safeguarding of a greater good. This represents a perpetual moral dilemma.

It seems unlikely that any general rule can be produced that would mark off the boundaries for each of the rights in question, and we are thus back at the inevitable conclusion that morality must function in actual situations, and the degree to which it functions successfully will determine the possibility of having certain principles hold sway. Any moral rule has its limitation, and the rights of the individual are needs limited by the rights of the collective. Some nations, such as France, would make this equation even stronger, stressing the primacy of the collective under any and all circumstances, while in other countries, such as the United States and Canada, individual rights have usually taken precedence.

Thus, extradition as well as asylum for terrorists are refugee issues that are clearly related to moral considerations, though it is difficult to establish a general rule about when refugee protection should prevail in such cases and when it should not.

Notes

1. In preceding pages Hathaway traces the development of the refugee concept as reflected in the international refugee definitions and the development of refugee law in general. He distinguishes between juridical, social and individual approaches to the definition of refugees, and emphasizes that while in the earlier stages refugees were defined in juridical terms (1920–35), later on (1935–39, during the Nazis persecutions) the definition had a social dimension. Thereafter the definition assumed an individualist perspective that rejected the determination of refugee status for whole groups or populations.

2. Exodus 12:49. The United States Constitution was interpreted in a similar fashion, although the right to deport an alien was maintained, as it was in Canada.

3. See Joseph Carens (1992).

4. For an analysis of this issue, see K. Hailbronner (1989), 67–79, and W. R. Brubaker (1989), 145–62.

5. Herbert Leuninger, speaking for ProAsyl, in personal conversation (May 1993). For more, see Chapter 10.

6. On this subject, see also A. MacIntyre (1988).

7. For a more complete listing, see Grahl-Madsen (1985, n. 54).

6

Through the Lens of Sociobiology

The Theory

Sociobiology is a relatively new inquiry into the way in which human beings function in their social settings. There is considerable apprehension that linkage of these two subjects denies the existence of free will and smacks of the nineteenth-century pseudo-science of phrenology or the Aryan supremacy doctrine of the Nazis. Lately, in Canada, certain theories have cast a shadow over enterprises of this sort. Professors C. Davison Ankney and Philippe Rushton have been the targets of broadside attacks for their research. Ankney's included measuring the differential brain size of men and women, and Rushton had concluded that there are differences in the levels of intelligence among Orientals, Caucasians, and Africans.

However, most sociobiological material is very different from Ankney's and Rushton's and deserves a hearing. It does not differentiate between various classes of human beings, but rather aims at exploring human nature as such.

It proceeds from the assumption that our genetic structures have been imprinted with a whole series of characteristics, capacities and drives that are common to all of us. For instance, every newborn child knows how to suckle its mother's breast, as does every newborn mammal. We know a great deal about animals and have observed such phenomena as innate fear, herd instincts and so forth.

Sociobiologists propose that human beings too react to each other in ways that have to do with our evolutionary development. We exhibit traits such as xenophobia and ethnocentrism which, while in part the result of education, may also be related to our humanness.[1]

This observation seems reasonable enough as a general proposition, but because of its apparent similarity to the pseudo-sciences of racial differentiation it has sometimes been put in the same class.[2] K. Kirkwood (1987) explains:

> There is evidence enough of the harm caused by over-confident and inadequate biological research, including the naive use by biologists of questionable historical and anthropological data. Even distinguished biologists heard seriously in this way were moving beyond their own area of specialization. Nevertheless, the reaction to such facts of those who, on ideological grounds, refuse even to concede that biological factors might deserve understanding is scarcely comprehensible. The nature-nurture controversy is far from resolved. Determination of the relative significance of hereditary and environmental factors among individuals and groups will continue to offer formidable and complex problems which are better dealt with by interdisciplinary respect and caution and the open sharing of data and hypotheses. The *ab initio* exclusion of students of sociobiology as a suspect out-group is unlikely to be helpful.

Irwin Silverman (1987, xv–xvi) also cautions against prejudgements of their attempt:

> Sociobiology is not a politically biased form of pseudo-science. It is not a movement of the far right—or any other political position. It is not politics dressed up as science. It is not naive science playing into the hands of political ideologues. Its proponents, those who think, talk and write about it, are not inevitably right-wing; indeed many would call themselves left-wing ... Some attempts to apply the sociobiological paradigm to human behavior have certainly been premature, ill-considered, superficial, overconfident, and indeed socio-politically naive ... The present book is not, however, yet another contribution to that general debate. It seeks to be a forward-looking, positive, sensitive and carefully balanced assessment of the arguments and evidence of biological and bio-psychological components in those areas of human action that are described by terms like prejudice, discrimination, in-group amity/out-group amity, xenophobia, and ethnocentrism.

The editors of *The Sociobiology of Ethnocentrism* (1987), Reynolds, Falger and Vines define ethnocentrism as a tendency to be unaware of the biases due to one's own makeup and the culture of one's own group, and to judge and interact with outsiders on the basis of those biases. Prejudice and discrimination, they say, are in essence the attitude and actions arising out of negative perceptions of members of other groups, subcultures or cultures, while "xenophobia is a psychological state of hostility or fear towards outsiders."

In-Groups and Out-Groups

The basic concepts of sociobiology were developed in the nineteenth century by anthropologist Edward Burnett Tylor (1832–1917) and sociologist William Graham Sumner (1840–1910).

According to Tylor, the dual nature of our relationship to others may be seen in the use of the Latin *hostis*. Basically, the word meant stranger as well as enemy, and as such one could relate to a *hostis* in a kindly fashion and become a host, or treat him as an enemy, hence with hostility. Violence towards one's own was different from violence against others.[3]

Tylor construed two types of social behaviour, a code of amity— leading to justice, honesty and veracity; and a code of enmity, leading to aggression, conquest and revenge.

It was Sumner who coined the words *ethnocentrism* and *xenophobia*, and who explained them in terms of warfare. War with the out-groups strengthens the in-group, whose members are not prone to struggle with each other in a time of crisis, lest they lose the war with the out-group. The latter is always seen as a possible enemy and therefore treated with suspicion; its members are strangers who at times are admitted and at other times fought.

Sumner therefore concluded that in order to be successful in war, a society must be at peace within itself and have a series of disciplines set up that will procure a quiescent social state. Rights develop out of this configuration: they keep the in-group peaceful and ready to fight the out-group. Consequently, there are two sets of rights: one for members of the in-group and one for the out-group.

W. D. Hammerman in 1964 enlarged the theory by linking it to fitness. According to him, genes must spread if their carriers are to increase not only their own fitness or reproductive success but also that of other individuals carrying the same genes. People's inclusive fitness is their personal fitness plus the increased fitness of relatives.[4]

Since the rejection or acceptance of refugees is indubitably related to the twin factors of xenophobia and ethnocentrism, a better understanding of these factors can aid us in our understanding of what, on the surface, appear to be politically and economically motivated reaction patterns.

Sociobiologists ask whether these feelings—which appear in all human societies—are part of an evolutionary process that sprang from our preference for relatives over strangers and created inherent patterns. Thus, do we pass on our concepts of superiority genetically, and do we use social markers—like hair, dress, badges and uniforms—merely to make clear at once who belongs to the group that inherently is ours? (Silverman 1987, xviii, ff.)

The obvious consequences of these markers are assumptions about ourselves and our likes as well as about others—assumptions that may be based on prejudice rather than knowledge. But having said this, the possibility still exists that these are essential components of our human structure, because we are all genetically ethnocentric. The sociobiologist agrees that xenophobia may be meliorated by education, cultural traditions and the like, but basically we would have to conclude that refugee acceptance runs against ingrained human structures.

In this regard a parallel to religion in general may be appropriately drawn, in that religious strictures and prohibitions tend to control to some degree such basic human drives as aggression and sexuality.

Sociobiologists would insist that all social activity has something to do with biology. Therefore, they would say, problems of refugees cannot be fully understood without reference to sociobiological insight.

According to Johan M. G. van der Dennen (1987, 1ff.), internal cohesion, relative peace, solidarity, loyalty and devotion to the in-group, and the glorification of one's own ideology, social myth, or one's own "God-given" social order are correlated with a state of hostility or permanent quasi-war towards out-groups, which are often perceived as inferior, subhuman and/or the incorporation of evil. Violence within the in-group is perceived as negative, violence with the out-group is heroic. Ethnocentrism manifests itself in either belligerence ("We are the best") or isolationism ("We are peaceful and can get along without others"). In the human realm there is a need to bond with others who are like-minded and to fight with those who are not.

What are the innate factors that produce these reactions? We have, together with most animals, a biological defence mechanism when we feel fear: we run away. But are the *reasons* for feeling fear innate as well? Van der Dennen (1987, 18) suggests:

> It appears possible for specific attitudes of hostility to be transmitted genetically in such a way that hostilities are directed towards strangers of one's own species to a greater extent than towards familiars of one's own species, or towards members of other species. It would not be impossible for xenophobia to be a partially innate attitude in the human.

Xenophobia may therefore be a normal aspect of human behaviour that can be changed by strong cultural training and the exercise of one's will. Translated into the realm of refugee acceptance, it would mean that spreading out the welcome mat is something we have to learn, similar to accepting the restrictive demands of religions, which run counter to biological impulses.

But while fear and inimical attitudes are thus related to biological factors, it seems more difficult to do the same with the opposite: the *acceptance* of the stranger. This acceptance has been called xenobiosis, which, according to Vincent Falger (1987, 247), is the "evolutionary stable inter-dependence ... relation in which colonies of one species live in the nests of another species and move freely among the hosts, obtaining food from them but still keeping their brood separate."

But, such theorists seem to take a large step in applying xenobiosis to human social behaviour. It would seem more promising to draw a parallel between xenobiosis and the basic structure of living cells, which depend on cooperation with other living cells in order to make the whole body survive. For group relations, such sociobiological parallels are plausible when dealing with in-groups, but, as a biological foundation for international cooperation and the acceptance of strangers, xenobiosis is not yet a persuasive theory. We would need hundreds of generations of the human species who have incorporated into their social structure the requirements and possibilities of the global village in order to create worldwide human interdependence—with rights and demands springing from it—to become part of our genetic structures.

The best argument for this transposition has been made by Robin I. M. Dunbar (1987), who relates the basic attitudes of hospitality—that is, the welcoming of strangers—to an individual's own survival instincts. For support, the author draws on basic human experiences. In certain cases, particularly in the desert, a stranger is often or even usually given food and shelter, Dunbar points out, adding, "This arrangement is strictly reciprocal in the sense that tolerance of strangers and a willingness to share food and shelter with them reflects an underlying recognition that travel in desert conditions would be all but impossible without such mutual arrangements."

But the argument is vitiated by the author's subsequent observation that the same desert tribes might rob or kill those same people when conditions are different, even after having extended unstinted hospitality to them. This appears to support those who believe that cultural influences rather than genetic designs have a more commanding impact on the formation of ethnocentrism and, one would conclude, on its opposite.

Application to Refugees

If strangers were originally seen as enemies, what happens to them when they are accepted as refugees? Sociobiologists speculate that human beings have predetermined degrees of sympathy. According to Ben W. Ike (1987, 216ff.), people are incapable of sympathizing with more than a limited number of their congeners, and this limited sympathy is a consequence of their evolution in small kin groups.

It is generally accepted that small groups were a common organizing phenomenon in early human history. Anthropological data indicate that whenever groups reached a critical mass—the upper level being 100, but usually 30 or 40—they would split into smaller groups. This phenomenon has been extensively investigated by Robert Ardrey, who concludes,

> There is an observation on modern life that, while preposterous in its proportions, cannot be neglected: Our juries include 11 members and a foreman. Our traditional army squad includes 11 soldiers and an officer. In the United States, we have nine Supreme Court Justices. Rare is the government, whatever its proliferation of ministries, in which more than nine, ten or eleven ministers combine actual power. Rare likewise is the contact sport, fielding a team of less than nine or more than eleven. The Soviet Union's Politburo has eleven members. It has been suggested to me that when Jesus chose his apostles he chose one too many.[5] (1987, 329–30)

The same analysis has been taken up by Karl Lorenz (1987), who speaks of the "eleven-man society" in which all people would steadfastly observe the Ten Commandments. But when the group gets larger our genetic programming is no longer sufficient to live up to the ideal code of behaviour. Perhaps this was the size of a typical group in early or pre-historic society.[6]

Studies of ancient warfare show that groups of nine to ten men constituted the basic fighting unit. Recent biblical research shows that the word *elef*—commonly understood as "1,000"—originally meant groups of nine or ten.[7]

From my own experience as a front-line soldier in World War II, I can attest to the fact that infantrymen who had been in our units for a fairly long time and who were grouped in small "buddy systems," were likely to have a better chance of survival than recent replacements that had not as yet been integrated into the "small sympathy group," to use Ike's terminology.

Everyone who has dealt with refugees and their problems knows that the passion we can muster on their behalf stands in direct relation to the number of refugees whose cases we take up. We are likely to invest a great deal of emotional capital and effort in one or two families whom we believe to have been wronged by the refugee admission process, but when our concern is with many or all refugees of a certain group, the intensity of our passion is diminished proportionately.

A telling example of this phenomenon occurred in August 1993. A five-year-old Bosnian girl, Irma Hadzimurativic, had been severely injured by shrapnel. The electronic media showed her plight and international attention was directed at her. She was flown to Great Britain for special care, and soon after hospitals in various countries offered to give attention to badly injured victims of the war.

Whereas previously the suffering of many thousands had failed to arouse compassion, one little girl's suffering was able to strike a sympathetic note, and in consequence war victims received badly needed treatment. But, those who benefited in this way were relatively few. Irma's case thus dramatically showed the possibilities and limitations of caring.

It is important to keep this human trait in mind, and whether or not sociobiologists can guide us in this regard, their conclusions should not be taken lightly. There seems to be an in-built limit to the sympathy that we can bring to bear on the problems of refugees, and for that reason it is essential to supplement our natural passion with strong moral convictions, which then must be incorporated into the legal framework of the nation. We cannot rely on the enlargement of human sympathy groups, for there is indeed good reason to believe that the inherent sympathy we can muster is biologically limited. Like religion, which in many respects is counterbiological, refugee advocacy must be grounded in educative efforts that take into consideration the natural obstacles that human groups present by the very fact that they are human.

Notes

1. Material for this chapter is taken primarily from a collection of essays entitled *The Sociobiology of Ethnocentrism* (1987), edited by V. Reynolds, V. Falger, I. Vine.

2. See Rose, Kamin and Lewontin (1984).

3. Tylor's understanding of the *lex talionis* was, however, flawed. He considered it only a primitive way of dealing with the consequences of violence, unaware that the law is also an expression of a significant legal development. For the latter, see Plaut (1981), 571ff.

4. Cited by Silverman (1987), xvii.

5. It is interesting to note that certain predators (like wolves) also hunt in packs of similar size.

6. Lorenz 1987, 150ff.; Ike 1987, 221. Adelman (1969, 98, 229) found this in university dormitories as well.

7. See Plaut 1981, 1034.

7

Community and Individual

Communitarianism

One of the founders of a new force in social self-perception is Amitai Etzioni (1990), who explains *communitarianism* as a social movement aimed at renewing the moral, social and political environment.

In his view, communal values and especially responsibilities have to countervail what he calls "radical individualism," as represented by such diverse groups as the American Civil Liberties Union and Evangelical Christians. Respect for individual rights must be balanced by the interests of the community, which combines responsibility with order and security. He criticizes the radical's preoccupation with individual rights, to the exclusion of responsibilities; it is this, he says, that destroys the sense of community.

Etzioni describes contemporary liberal philosophers as "cut off from all social moorings," and criticizes them for their "lifeless, impoverished conception of community and the common good." Communitarians, on the other hand, believe that "the shared moral values, 'virtues', and traditions of the community, rather than the rational choices of abstract individuals, are the bedrock of moral-philosophical discourse" (1990, 216–18).

He and his followers thus broadly speak of morality, family and other social values, rather than of economic rearrangements. They are generally suspicious of governments that handle communal concerns, such as Medicare, public broadcasting or public transportation, and would rather that they address the need for a clean environment, the promotion of good health, safe streets, an informed citizenry and opposition to crime.

Given this framework, communitarians are likely to have problems with an emphasis on the rights of individual refugees, and instead underscore the rights of the receiving community to maintain its standard of living, its cultural identity and heritage. Thus, they would tend to restrict or exclude refugees and still be able to claim the high ground of morality.

But at the same time, Etzioni criticizes those communitarians like Walzer who, in his view, do not protect individual rights sufficiently. To him, the community and the individual have rights that are not derived from each other, and therefore they need mutual respect and accommodation. Instead of the "We and They" thinking that pits residents against strangers, he posits the "I and We" image, which bespeaks cooperation, understanding and compassion, and does not lead to confrontation and xenophobia. It is built on the concept of what he calls a responsive community that appeals to values that members already possess and encourages them to internalize values they currently do not have (Etzioni 1990, 227).

Etzioni does not speak here of refugees, but that paradigm is compelling. A responsive community is one that appeals to the best of human impulses and affirms values that are persuasive rather than coercive.

Membership

The concept of *membership*, prominently developed by Michael Walzer (1983), has been used to narrow the concept of asylum. The concept itself is a late-twentieth-century update of Rousseau's *contrat social*.

Walzer compares the state to a kind of enlarged club: you become a member by the agreement of those already affiliated, and they will decide whether you "fit." Those who are members are bound together by a pact of mutual aid, distributing justice and exchanging social goods. Occasionally, strangers might be entitled to the group's hospitality, and this will frequently be extended if the need is very great and if—most importantly—the risks and costs of giving aid are relatively low for the members. Walzer compares this to hospitality extended by a single person or a family. He says, "I need not take the injured stranger into my home, except briefly, and I certainly need not care for him or even associate with him for the rest of my life" (1983, 33).

The membership concept counters a global libertarianism that posits the theory that once upon a time all people were partners in a global "state" and membership was *ab initio* distributed equally. Walzer criticizes this concept as unrealistic and unworkable.

Whom then would communitarians wish to invite as members? Admission policy, according to Walzer, would be based on

a. political/economic considerations;
b. the character and destiny of the host country; and
c. the character of the political community/country (which presupposes that the members have a fair idea of what constitutes their country).

Membership in the state cannot be compared with that in a neighbourhood, for people usually move into neighbourhoods of their own accord and do not require or request the agreement of those already living there. Walzer cites Henry Sidgewick who, as long ago as 1881, suggested that if we conceived of the global society as a world of neighbourhoods, there would be neither internal cohesion nor a sense of patriotism.

Taking up Sidgewick's analogy of neighbourhoods, Walzer proposes the following alternative:

> A country that has an open admissions policy and therefore will become one large neighborhood, will develop small neighborhoods which then become quasi-states like China Town or Little Italy, and which will bond to protect themselves against strangers and establish closed or parochial communities. Thus, neighborhoods are open if states are closed, and if states are open neighborhoods are closed.
>
> Only if the states make a selection among would-be members and guarantee the loyalty, security and welfare of the individuals they select, can local communities take shape as "indifferent" associations, determined solely by personal preference and market capacity ... The restraint of entry serves to defend the liberty and welfare, the politics and culture of a group committed to one another and to their common life. But the restraint of [emigration] replaces commitment with coercion. (1983, 38–39)

To be sure, the states will convince their members that they are acting morally and in defence of shared values, to protect their identity as well as their standard of living. Needless to say, such concepts have fueled propositions to restrict asylum for the sake of maintaining the identity of membership.

Walzer further compares the admission of immigrants and refugees with the admission of new members to a club. Both encourage family ties. Clubs encourage members to enrol their children, thereby to assure the sense of "fit," and similarly states promote the kinship principle by giving priority to the immigration of relatives of recent arrivals to whom they have extended permanent residence.

Walzer cites Australia as a prime example of an attempt to create a membership state. Australians had aimed at fashioning a homogeneous nation. But a major problem arose when the vast areas of unoccupied land the continent possessed were said to be part of the nation's homogeneity, and settling strangers in such desolate areas was never seriously addressed during immigration policy debates. (Meanwhile, the borders were opened slightly to immigrants and refugees of various backgrounds.)

The whole concept of membership is subject to moral queries, for every state is a member of the community of nations and therefore shares the responsibility of shaping an orderly world, and this includes the responsibility to eliminate the causes that produce refugees.

Generally, nations feel a responsibility towards persecuted people who are essentially "like them." Thus Canadian and American doors were wide open for Czechs and Hungarians, but not for Afghans or Angolans. Furthermore, morality seems to stand in direct relation to the number of people involved:

> So long as the number of victims is small, mutual aid will generate similar practical results; and when the number increases, and we are forced to choose amongst the victims, we will look rightfully for some more direct connection with our own way of life. Communities must have boundaries, and however these are determined with regard to territory and resource, they depend with regard to population on a sense of relatedness and mutuality. Refugees must appeal to that sense. One wishes them success, but in particular cases, with reference to a particular state, they may well have no right to be successful. (Walzer 1983, 49–50)

Would an international authority that has greater power than the United Nations High Commissioner for Refugees be effective in loosening the rules of membership? Perhaps, says Walzer, it would do better to focus on intervention against states whose brutal policies drive their own citizens into exile, and thus enable them to go home. He maintains the basic right of a political community to shape its own population and to maintain the meaning of membership for the sake of current members and the principle of mutual aid among them. In sum, "admission and exclusion are at the core of communal independence" (1983, 62).

Refugee admission, therefore, is a matter of political choice and necessity on the one hand, and moral constraint on the other. But Walzer insists that all states have basic membership characteristics and the responsibility it has to its citizens to maintain the right to determine who is and who is not to be admitted is one of its foundations.[1] How all of this squares with the nation's adherence to international conventions that deal with refugees is another matter.

One of Walzer's critics is Joseph Carens (1987a), who believes that the comparison of states to clubs is flawed, for states are public and clubs are private—an essential distinction. Public institutions must practise equal treatment, while clubs, being private, are able to pick and choose their members as they wish. The latter's admission policies are not appropriate for states, which must treat individuals equally.

There is little question that communitarian theories give the current practices of most states their theoretical foundation. It is the accepting community that determines whether permanent or temporary asylum is to be granted or not. The applicant has no right to it, and the UN Convention indeed validates that point. For the refugees, their only right is not to be returned to a threatening condition, but this right does affect whether one is accepted for permanent asylum.

Communitarianism is primarily an idea, a way of thinking rather than a policy. An updating of Burke's approval of tradition, it is sufficiently supported as a serious new category of thinking about society. For refugees, hope lies in a compromise between the needs of the host community and their own needs. That compromise alone provides a framework for moral action.

Germany as the Paradigm

The communitarian debate was brought to the world's attention by the 1992–93 anti-foreigner riots in Germany. The question asked there as elsewhere was and has been: can we allow refugees to change our country's character? The prevalent answer then and since then has been that naturalization should be granted only when the applicant is thoroughly integrated into German society and/or has sufficient public support. There is general agreement that the character of German society must not be altered (whatever precisely that may mean), and that therefore ethnic Germans should be allowed to be naturalized quickly. Also, membership in political or emigrant organizations that have ties to the home country of the applicant is considered evidence against a permanent attachment to Germany.

Kay Hailbronner claims that the Federal Republic of Germany is not a melting pot, because the nation is "relatively small and overcrowded" and wants to ensure a reasonable amount of homogeneity of cultural and political outlook. Therefore, tough naturalization laws have kept even long-term immigrants and their German-born children at the status of residents rather than German citizens. Religion too has been at issue:

> Freedom of religion ... does not include the right to agitate and exercise heavy-handed pressure to alter the values and behavior of the foreign population in a way that runs against efforts to insure their social integration. (1989, 69)

Hailbronner sees Germany as the perfect example of the communitarian approach to membership:

> Political communities formed for self-preservation of the protection and advancement of common interests or united by shared historical experience will entrust power only to those persons from whom they can expect a feeling of solidarity and loyalty ... who can be expected to share common interests.[2] (1989, 75)

Germans, therefore, perceive themselves as a nation that cannot become a permanent country of asylum and immigration. But Germany is not the only country that sees itself in this light. To one degree or another, most refugee receiving nations have similar views of themselves.

Clearly, a middle ground must be found between communitarians and refugee advocates. Unrestricted immigration or refugee flows are no longer possible, and certainly not in Western countries. High-flown ideals that would allow each refugee a secure place of asylum have foundered on the shoals of the latest developments.

A New Norm: Nonentrée

In a trenchant article, James C. Hathaway (1993) claimed that the traditional concentration of refugee law on nonrefoulement has become outdated. The time is gone, he averred, when the nonreturn of refugees to their places of origin was a chief content of refugee legislation. No longer: today the issue is the refugee's opportunity to find asylum, not the secondary question of nonrefoulement which arises only after asylum has been found. "If we examine the current practice of states," he says, "particularly but not exclusively those in the developed world, we can see ... that nonrefoulement is being displaced by a new norm of non-entrée: the refugee shall not access our community."

The tools assuring nonentrée are well known: from sanctions imposed on airline companies if they do not require proper identification before boarding their passengers, all the way to stationing armed guards at borders with instructions to turn refugee claimants away. Hathaway also puts into this category the concentration of Haitian asylum seekers at the American military base in Guantanamo, Cuba; the creation of a "safe haven" for Kurds within Iraq; or the creation of a no-man's-land at French airports where arrivals are segregated and considered not to have entered France at all.

"Why", Hathaway writes, "is non-entrée effectively replacing nonrefoulement as the corner stone of contemporary international law? From the perspective of states, its appeal is that it permits states to exercise *control* over refugee movements without also assuming *responsibility* for their welfare, as admissions to that state's community would imply." Why, moreover, has this development taken place at the end of the twentieth century? Because, says Hathaway, original refugee law was concerned with and could focus on individuals. That is no longer so, because of the huge masses of refugees who seek asylum. Where refugee legislation continues to sort out whether individual claimants satisfy the conditions of the Geneva Convention, the backlog grows, as does the waiting period; people live in limbo and do not know whether they have been accepted or not, and when it will ever be possible to be reunited with their families.

In fact, the old categories of refugee legislation were put in place under the assumption that asylum seekers were from "related" countries and could easily integrate in the nation that offered asylum. But with hundreds of thousands of refugees from the Third World knocking at Western doors, the issue of relatedness no longer applies. It is Hathaway's thesis that this dichotomy has shifted refugee law from nonrefoulement to nonentrée.

> It is the "differentness" of these refugees, not just their numbers which troubles Northern governments. Authorities argue, increasingly openly, that the admission of counter-entropic minorities threatens the social solidarity of communities in developed states, and can therefore legitimately be resisted.[3]

Thus, nonentrée becomes the paradigm for the basic question: may a state restrict refugee movements because in the absence of such restriction the nature of the receiving state might be radically altered? This is the question of "membership," which pits communitarian advocates against those who want to uphold individual rights. Clearly the ground has shifted, as has the debate over what constitutes a moral basis for granting or refusing asylum.

Notes

1. Walzer's ideas are also advanced by Schuck and Smith (1985).
2. This, of course, was also claimed by Nazism and fascism, both of which sailed under the flag of community values, which asserted a prior claim to loyalty.
3. That sentiment is not new. See the story of Canada turning back the steamship *St. Louis* (Abella and Troper, 1982, 63–64). See also Chapter 12 in Abella and Troper.

8

Contended Rights:
To Leave, Return, Remain

The Right to Leave

Next to the initial creation of refugees, the unwillingness of other states to admit them, is indubitably the most urgent problem. Yet, in a strange way it has its counterpart in the unwillingness of some nations to let those members of their own populations who wish to, leave the country. For the state controls both who may enter and also who may leave. The prohibition to leave may be termed a refugee problem in reverse, of the kind known more popularly as the plight of the *refuseniks,* a term coined to describe Jews in the Soviet Union who applied for permission to leave for Israel, but were refused their exit visas. This refusal was of course a direct contravention of Article 13 of the Universal Declaration of Human Rights: "Everyone has the right to leave any country, including his own, and to return to his country."

In the past, governments could not control the exit or entrance of people as tightly as they can today. Further, a major restriction on the freedom to move in any direction was limited by slavery and servitude. Some examples are: in the thirteenth century B.C.E., an Egyptian ruler tried to prevent the exodus of his Hebrew slaves;[1] in the seventeenth and eighteenth centuries, some European states outlawed emigration in order to increase their own population base; and in the twentieth century some states (especially those belonging to the former Soviet bloc) required their populations to remain as a matter of pride and integrity, proclaiming it to be a form of treason to leave the socialist "paradise." The most egregious cruelties arising from this policy were the shootings at the Berlin Wall.[2]

There are states which force some people to leave, while others are forced to stay. Thus, in the 1980s, Afghan doctors and professionals were not allowed to leave, whereas villagers in towns of antigovernment military activity were made to flee—creating the strange contrast that mass expulsions were coupled with tight restrictions on exits. In all these instances the key is the individual's usefulness to the state, while issues of personal freedom have little or no importance.[3] As one commentator has said,

> It is modern ideologies that have perfected the idea that the interest of the state, assumed to represent society as a whole, should take priority over individual whim and caprice. According to the collectivist ethic, the burden is on individuals to demonstrate why they should be allowed to leave, rather than the state to show why they should not. This line of reasoning simply concludes that the happiness of the whole is better served if individuals are compelled to remain a part of it. (Dowty 1987, 10)

Leaving or not leaving one's country becomes in fact a mirror of the social contract:

> The right to leave thus gets at the very essence of government by consent—a concept that has achieved near universal acceptance in principle, even amongst states that rarely abide by it. Since government by consent holds that citizenship is a voluntary act, the right to leave a country implicitly serves to ratify the contract between an individual and society. If a person who has the right to leave chooses to stay, he has signaled his voluntary acceptance of the social contract. From this follows his obligation to society. But if he does not have the option of leaving, then society's hold on him is based only on coercion.
>
> Thus the state in all too many instances became a prison and the right to leave the last refuge of liberty. (Dowty 1987, 15ff.)

Clearly, the right to leave a country is intimately bound up with the whole concept of the right to self-determination. Its restriction is one more example of the claim to total sovereignty that states arrogate to themselves. The individual lives by grace of the collective and not, as in Rousseau's vision, the other way around.

The Right to Return

For some forty-five years Palestinian refugees have demanded the right to return to their former places of habitation, which are now inside the State of Israel. To back up their demand, they have cited a variety of legal documents and principles, and resolutions of the UN; the Israelis, in refusing the wholesale return of at least two million refugees, have cited their own right of survival as a nation. The result is a classic conflict that has pitted two rights against each other. Each side claims the superiority of its claim, and the result is a stand-off, which six wars have not been able to solve.

The Palestinian position may be set forth as follows: the partition of November 29, 1947, passed by the General Assembly of the United Nations (resolution 181), divided what was then the Palestine Mandate of Great Britain into Jewish and Arab areas. The resolution made no reference to the Palestinians' repeated demand for the maintenance of the integrity of their country and for its independence within its constituted boundaries. The resolution thus was seen to undermine the Palestinians' right to self-determination, since by a stroke of the international pen it deprived those living in the area allotted to Jews of their right to choose their own political identity.

The resolution included the following specific rights and provisions, however:

1. Arabs retained their right to live in their homes, towns and villages;
2. They were not to be discriminated against;
3. Their adequate primary and secondary education was to be insured; and
4. Their property was not to be expropriated except for clear public purposes.

The problem was that even though the Jews accepted the partition and its considerations, the Arabs did not and war broke out, with seven Arab nations marshalling their forces against the Jewish population, which at that time numbered only some 600,000 people. The Arabs were defeated in the conflict, and on May 14, 1948, the Jews proclaimed the existence of the State of Israel.

During the war many Arabs fled their habitations. Why this happened has been hotly debated. Did Israel force the Arabs out or did most of them leave their homes at the request of their own leadership who promised them an early return after the Jewish entity had been annihilated? Benny Morris (1988 and 1990) holds a middle position: no design created the problem, but war itself.[4] During a war people are killed (even though killing is ordinarily prohibited); people are displaced; and when the outcome of the war creates new conditions and boundaries, rarely returned to their original condition. The separation of some twelve million Germans from their homes at the end of World War II resulted in what appears to have been their permanent displacement. There is little question that Poland would not readmit any large number of them, because doing so would likely undermine the existence of its own nation. Here too the right of return has been claimed, and here too self-preservation has made its counterclaim.

Resolution no. 194 (III) of December 11, 1948, passed by the General Assembly of the United Nations, stated:

> 11. ... that the refugees wishing to return to their homes and live at peace with their neighbours should be permitted to do so at the earliest practical date, and that compensation should be paid for. The property of those choosing not to return and for the loss of or damage to property which, under principles of international law or in equity, should be made good by the Governments of authorities responsible ...

Both Arabs and Israelis cite this resolution as fundamental: the Arabs stress both the right to return and compensation, while the Israelis emphasize that the premise of this article—that neighbours must live peaceably with each other—has not yet been fulfilled.

Now, more than four decades later, it seems futile to speculate as to what would have happened if both parties had accepted the UN resolution. Would a refugee problem have arisen at all? Israelis claim it would not; Arab analysts hold that the question is a trap, because the UN resolution itself was illegal.

Resolution 242, adopted by the Security Council on November 22, 1967, in the wake of the Six-Day War, which was reaffirmed by resolution 363, has become the instrument to which both parties refer. However, for Israelis, resolution 242 is considered a sufficient basis for future arrangements, while Arabs generally see it as insufficient—a beginning rather than an end.

Arabs point to the fact that in 1969 the United Nations declared that the Palestinian Arabs were a separate people with a right to self-determination. This became a premise of subsequent UN resolutions. A resolution of November 30, 1970, for example, concluded that the Palestinians, because they had the right to self-determination, had the right also to "struggle to achieve their right of self-determination by any means at their disposal."

The United Nations proceeded to support four major Palestinian issues: the right to return, the right to self-determination, the right to struggle and the right to receive aid in their struggle.

In 1978 the United Nations published *The Right of Return of the Palestinian People*, edited by the Committee on the Exercise of the Inalienable Rights of the Palestinian People. The book presents the historical development of the above-noted principle of the right of return. Its authors trace this principle to Plato, whom they quote to demonstrate that he affirmed the right of any person to his property, regardless of its location.

Further supporting quotations are from the Magna Carta, the French Constitution of 1791, and other documents and authors. To be sure, in all these instances the rights accorded to people adhere to individuals rather than to whole nations and groups.

The authors believe that such precedents are backed by a moral force unchallenged in international relations, and they elevate the right of return to a fundamental human right and, as such, affirm that it is a binding international principle.

There can be little doubt that the individual's right to return has been supported in many political as well as international instruments. Why then would the Israelis, who pride themselves on living in a democratic state, deny Arabs this right? Their defence may be summarized as follows:

To begin with, it should be noted that the right of return is not acknowledged by everyone. Thus Israel's former Minister of External Affairs, Abba Eban, once wrote: "Membership in the United Nations is based on the principle of the sovereign equality of all its members. This means that Israel's control of entry to its territory is equivalent to that of the United States, the USSR, Egypt or any of the other 150 and more member states ..."[5]

Israel has considered the above-noted UN resolutions and their interpretations as devoid of any meaning. They were adopted, say Isrealis, at a time when the Arab/Israeli confrontation had become a part of the East/West tension, and in the United Nations, the Soviet Union had the automatic support of most Third World countries, resulting in resolutions that sometimes had little to do with reality but everything to do with politics. Thus in 1977, the United Nations declared that Zionism was a form of racism—a resolution that was promptly reversed once the Soviet/American confrontation had ceased to be a factor.

Israelis further claim that at the very time when some 800,000 Palestinians were displaced, a similar number of Jews were also displaced from Arab countries. But while the latter were integrated in

Israel and given a home, many Palestinian refugees were discouraged or prevented from integrating into the Arab countries to which they had fled. They were kept from becoming part of the resident population because the maintenance of refugee camps was deemed to be a potent means of political pressure on Israel. Integration would have negated the claim that return was urgent, but in this fashion the problem has been successfully kept alive for forty-five years. Israelis therefore ask: even if 800,000 to a million Jews were willing to return to Syria and North Africa, would they be accepted and would their property be restored to them? In their view an exchange of populations has already taken place, and this as much as anything is part of the present reality and has to be taken into account.

Israelis make one further point. They assert that it has been the inability or unwillingness of the surrounding Arab states (except for Egypt) to recognize Israel's right to existence and to make peace with the Israelis, that has rendered Israel incapable of accommodating the refugees, even if it were willing to do so under normal circumstances. The Arab states in their turn say that they would be ready to accommodate Israel, but the refugee problem must be solved before they would be willing to take this step. Whether or not the September 1993 agreement between Israel and the PLO will substantially tackle the refugee problem remains to be seen.

The agreement provides for consideration in stages; refugees from the 1967 (Six-Day) war will receive attention in the first two years of the accord; the displacements occasioned by the 1947–48 war would be part of arrangements scheduled to take place after 1995. The peace process begun in Madrid also affords the opposing parties the possibility of direct relief for refugees through the UN Multilateral Working Group on Refugees.

Palestinians criticize and Israelis endorse the Law of Return, which Israel enacted on July 5, 1950, at the very beginning of its national existence. It began with the statement: "Every Jew has the right to come to this country as an *oleh* [defined as a Jew coming to Israel for settlement] ..." This law was in effect a declaration that explained the reason for Israel's very existence: a people of refugees for the last two thousand years was at last to have a place where they could go as a right and not by the sufferance of any nation that could reserve the right to grant or refuse them admission. From now on, Diaspora Jews could still become refugees (as indeed would be the case in such countries as the former Soviet Union from the 1970s on), but that status would end automatically upon their arrival in Israel.

Palestinian refugees claim that the Law of Return thus discriminates against them: Jews who have never before set foot on the land are permitted and even encouraged to come and settle, while they, who have lived there for generations, are denied the right of return.

The persistent difficulty of the confrontation is that it is no one-sided refugee problem (one group, which has been displaced, seeking admission or readmission), but a two-sided one: Israel is faced with refugees of two types, Jews and non-Jews. Its existence is bound up with the necessary admission of the former and thus it is not discriminatory in the ordinary sense, but rather in the existential sense. But that proposition did not allow for the possibility that in the conflict that attended the creation of the state there would also be refugees who would enter their own claim to return to the land.

Israelis point out that the word "return" has a different meaning for the two peoples involved. For the Jews it means leaving a position of minority status, insecurity and often bitter persecution in the lands of the Diaspora and claiming their ancient heritage to live in their own land. They say that Arabs on the other hand are no such minority; they already live in countries that are fully Arab and Muslim[6]. Their desire is to reclaim their habitat and their property, while the Jews' return is motivated differently.

Today, underlying all Israeli arguments is one prime consideration: the return of more than a million Arabs, many of them radicalized and bitterly opposed to the very existence of Israel, would pose a mortal danger to the state. Self-preservation, as the Israelis see it, has priority over all else, including the right of Palestinians to wholesale return.

Of late, the confrontation has been fueled by growth in the numbers of extremists on both sides. These extremists are driven by religious convictions and reject the claim of the other as a matter of principle. The Muslim rejectionists, among whom Hamas has become a standard bearer, has attained increasing support amongst Arabs in Gaza and the West Bank. The *intifada* (the Palestinian uprising) highlighted the inherent and seemingly insoluble conflict.

A massacre committed by an American Jewish physician in 1994 had an enormous impact on both sides. He belonged to one of the right-wing/religious Kach groups who hold that a truly Jewish state could not be a democracy, and that therefore Arabs would have to leave Israel either voluntarily or involuntarily in order to secure Jewish existence in the country or, if they chose to stay, would have to agree to a separate status.

Withal, an increasing recognition that the proclamation of rights in and of itself cannot claim sole possession of morality has taken hold. If this confrontation of rights is perceived in "either-or" terms there can be no peaceable solution. Accommodation must be made.

In sum, two rights are in conflict, and there are but three possible ways of dealing with it: maintenance of the status quo, war or political accommodation. The first two have not worked in the past and have engendered further conflicts; only the last has any chance of success. Hopefully, the mutual recognition of Israel and the Palestine Liberation Organization will, despite the seemingly continuous violence, result in tangible steps for a just and permanent, negotiated settlement of the refugee problem.

The Right to Remain

In early 1993 the United Nations High Commissioner for Refugees, Sadako Ogata, addressed the Commission of Human Rights. Excerpts from the talk will serve to strike a new note in the field of refugee protection. They are presented here without comment, for they need none:

> The issue of human rights and the problems of refugees are so inextricably linked that it is hardly possible to discuss one without referring to the other. Human rights violations are a major cause of refugee flows and also a major obstacle to the solution of refugee problems through voluntary repatriation.
>
> More positively, safeguarding human rights is the best way to prevent conditions that force people to become refugees; respect for human rights is a key element in the protection of refugees in their country of asylum; and improved observance of human rights standards is often critical for the solution of refugee problems by enabling refugees to return safely home ...
>
> Like refugees, the internally displaced are in a very vulnerable situation. Like refugees, they need protection, assistance, and a solution to their plight. Although the UNHCR does not have a general mandate for the internally displaced, the interrelationship between their situation and that of refugees has meant UNHCR is frequently called upon to assume responsibilities on their behalf, particularly in situations where the need for humanitarian assistance is coupled with a need for protection ...

Frequently, the internally displaced cannot obtain effective protection from their own government, either because it has lost control of a part of its territory or because it perceives them as a threat and supports or condones violations of their rights. Since they have not left their country, the internally displaced do not qualify for international protection as refugees. Their protection needs must be met through the general provisions of human rights and humanitarian law, and through *ad hoc* operational arrangements. How to secure observance of the norms of human rights and humanitarian law for the internally displaced is one of the most important challenges facing the international community ...

The prevention of refugee flows and of internal displacement requires protecting the right of people to remain in safety in their homes. There are unfortunately too many instances where human rights have been or are being deliberately violated with the aim of expelling whole groups of people from their homes and from their country. The former Yugoslavia provides a particularly graphic and painful example. There, UNHCR is providing assistance not only to refugees and the displaced, but also to people who are under a direct threat of expulsion either through military attack or through the form of persecution referred to as "ethnic cleansing." The atrocities that are the instruments of this policy include murder, torture, mutilation and rape. Despite all our efforts they continue even now. And this unfortunately is only one example of the threats worldwide to the human right to remain.

In speaking of "the right to remain," I mean to underline the need to protect the basic right of the individual not to be forced into exile and emphasize an aspect of human rights that serves further development in connection with our efforts to address the cause of refugee flight. The right to remain is implicit in the right to leave one's country and to return there. In its simplest form it could be said to include the right to freedom of movement and residence within one's own country. It is inherent in Article 9 of the Universal Declaration of Human Rights that no one shall be subject to arbitrary exile. It is linked also to other fundamental human rights because when people are forced to leave their homes, a whole range of other rights are threatened, including the right to life, liberty and security of the person, non-discrimination, the right not to be subjected to torture or degrading treatment, the right to privacy and family life.

If I, as the High Commissioner of Refugees, emphasized the right not to become a refugee, it is because I know that the international protection the UNHCR, in cooperation with countries of asylum, can offer to refugees is not an adequate substitute for the protection that they should have received from their own governments in their own countries. This generosity of asylum countries cannot fully replace the loss of a homeland or relieve the pain of exile. In this period of heightened tension between various groups within countries and growing threats of conflicts whose primary aim is to force one group of people to leave territory shared with another, the question of how to enforce people's right to remain, to have their rights respected where they are, and not have to flee to find protection, has become urgent. I invite you to consider human rights situations from the standpoint of the right to remain because I am convinced that there will be no end to the plight of refugees until the international community has found ways to deal effectively with the root cause of forced displacement ... (Ogata 1993, II)

Notes

1. Exodus Chapter 5ff.
2. See Dowty (1987), 1ff.
3. Dowty (1987, 8–11) cites Plato as one who endorses the right of the community to control the exit of its citizens. On the other hand, Dowty says, Delphic priests felt that unrestricted movement was one of the four freedoms separating liberty from slavery.
4. Morris (1988, 286). He is the scholar most often cited in discussions of this point, though he is not unopposed.
5. *Jerusalem Post International*, August 1989. The danger of a wholesale return of Arabs, threatening the very destruction of Israel, is discussed in *Spectrum*, May/June 1992.
6. Note the Kuwaitis' desire to return at the end of the Gulf War.

PART TWO:

The Practice

9

Refugees in Africa

Open Borders Amidst Poverty

In 1993, Adelman summarized the refugee problem in Africa as follows:

> Refugees and Africa seem almost synonymous. Of the over fifteen million in the world, Africa has more than five million. They are the product of ideological wars and nationalist conflicts, of environmental disasters and ethnic hatreds, of the brutal ambition for power of a few and the poverty of many ... In no other continent is there such vast suffering. In no other continent do we find greater generosity in the local assistance given to refugees by surrounding states. They have a broader definition of a refugee and the obligations to assist, yet in some places the conflicts are so horrendous and the terrain so formidable that aid agencies cannot overcome the military and geographic obstacles to deliver needed relief supplies. In no other continent are the needs so vast and the capacity to assist so meager. (1993, vii)

Africa is a continent of many traditions, religions, and political realities. Largely beset by poverty, nevertheless it shoulders much of the refugee burden. It is generally assumed that the roots of this accepting treatment of others rests on tribal traditions of hospitality that compare favourably with the more formalized sense of obligation customary in the West. In the following pages, "Africa" is used as a kind of collective description which, of course, does not mean to overlook the significant differences existing in its multinational mosaic.

It will be helpful to look at the Conference on Legal, Economic and Social Aspects of African Refugee Problems, which was held in 1976, and was attended by representatives from twenty-one African countries, ten international and intergovernmental organizations, as well as representatives of a few non-African countries.[1]

Though the Conference agreed on a Convention document which dealt with pragmatic issues, one must be struck by its constant reference to moral duties. Among the recommendations made were: expansion of the refugee concept; continuation of a liberal policy towards asylum; and the general principle that anyone on a nation's territory deserves protection. The Convention also recommended that African states be guided by the following principles in the granting of asylum:

1. African States shall use their best endeavors consistent with their laws and constitutions to admit all refugees and to promote the settlement of those refugees who, for well-founded reasons, do not wish to return to their country of origin or nationality. [Note the term "well-founded reasons," which is very broad and not limited as in the UN declaration.]

2. The grant of asylum to refugees is a peaceful and humanitarian act and shall not be regarded as an unfriendly act by an African State.

3. No person shall be subjected by an African State to measures such as rejection at the frontier, return or expulsion, which would compel him to remain in or return to a territory where his life, physical integrity or liberty would be threatened ...

4. When an African State finds difficulty in continuing to grant asylum to refugees, other African States should consider, in a spirit of African solidarity and international cooperation, appropriate measures to lighten the burden of the African State granting asylum.

5. If a refugee has not received the right to reside in any country, he shall have a claim to temporary residence in the country of asylum in which he first presented himself as a refugee, pending arrangements for his resettlement ...

6. Every refugee owes a duty to the country of asylum, which requires in particular that he conforms to its laws and regulations as well as to measures taken for the maintenance of public order. He shall also abstain from any subversive activities against any African country, except for countries under colonial and racist minority domination.[2]

Colonial Memories[3]

Before the colonial period and for some time after, a non-African stranger could usually move freely from one place to another and temporarily resettle. But in the Black-White confrontation, feelings towards strangers have changed from friendliness to ambivalence, indifference, fear and antagonism.

Some authors, in particular Shack and Skinner (1979), therefore contradict the general impression that Africa has been and still is hospitable and unreservedly amicable towards strangers. Rather, they say, "newcomers are seldom welcomed anywhere on the same social terms as indigenous members of the society."

It would seem, however, that to a significant degree this resistance to strangers is a reaction to White people who in the past were in positions of dominance, and that this sentiment was carried over to Asian strangers as well. The 1970 expulsion in Uganda of Kenyans and, two years later, of Asians was justified by dictator Idi Amin as a consequence of their social and/or political power. It was as well a function of the class structure in that country—observable among other African societies—which lacked the capacity to accommodate outsiders and therefore became inhospitable. Added thereto were myths and stereotypes regarding strangers. Shack and Skinner (1979, 44) claim that much of this incapacity was traceable to differences of economic status: strangers were usually entrepreneurs and middlemen. In countries where immigrant strangers did not acquire significant wealth (such as Ethiopia) the overt hostility observable elsewhere has been largely absent. Margaret Peil comments similarly:

> A "stranger" [in Ghana] may have many friends from various groups ... and be indistinguishable in dress or behavior from others in the neighborhood; but there is almost always a reserve, an attitudinal and emotional distance which makes it clear that he remains at least partly a stranger.[4]

Harsh Realities

Some years ago, African refugee movements were summarized by Zdenek Cervenka in this way:

> There are two categories of refugees in Africa—those from dependent territories and those from independent African States. The first category is closely connected with the liberation efforts directed against the remaining colonial regimes in Africa, notably the Portuguese. It also includes the refugees from South Africa and Rhodesia [Zimbabwe], as neither country is exactly independent in the eyes of Africans, but represents a white minority regime oppressing the African majority,

the position of the latter being little different from that of the refuges
from dependent territories. (1969, 94ff.)

Thus, persons engaged in political activity or even armed struggle
against colonial powers were considered freedom fighters, and therefore, upon arrival in another state, they were seen as refugees. Also,
those who left such countries in search of jobs or social betterment and
better educational facilities were generally considered refugees—a
fundamental difference from the United Nations definition which is
common guideline for most refugee receiving countries.

However, even in this postcolonial age, massive population problems exist in many parts of Africa. They are usually attributable to
victims of political or tribal persecution or persons engaged in activities
directed against the regnant government. This in turn creates a dilemma for the refugee-receiving nation—as in the West—for if such
persons are recognized as refugees they might thereby disturb diplomatic relations between otherwise friendly nations, despite Article 2 of
the above-noted 1976 Convention and the earlier Accra resolution
adopted by the Organization of African Unity (OAU), entitled "The
Problem of Refugees in Africa." In that resolution, the OAU said that it

- *Reaffirms* its desire to give all possible assistance to refugee
  from any Member State on a humanitarian and fraternal
  basis,
- *Recalls* that Member States have pledged themselves to
  prevent refugees living on their territories from carrying out
  by any means whatsoever any acts harmful to the interests
  of other States, Members of the Organization of African
  Unity,
- *Requests* all Member States never to allow the refugee question to become a source of dispute amongst them ...[5]

No solutions to these problems seem to be in sight. In Liberia many
citizens have been uprooted and many of them have become casualties
of a brutal war; refugees from Sierra Leone have been internally
displaced; starving Ethiopians wandered en masse into the Sudan,
itself a poverty stricken country; and Somalis fled to wherever there
was hope of getting a slice of bread.[6] [As this book was going to press,
a bloody civil war in Rwanda produced additional large numbers of
refugees.]

The help received by these refugees—the term is used in the African
sense—was often minimal or even nonexistent, but borders were

generally not closed to them. In this respect the poorest nations in the world have set a significant example for the richest. To be sure, African tribal, linguistic and ethnic traditions have played some role in this regard, but in the end this fact is incontrovertible: for whatever reasons, most African states have not practised the exclusionary tactics used in the West. They are not closing their borders or applying refugee definitions that would make it impossible for those fleeing hunger or civil war to establish themselves in a new environment.

A Dissonant View

The view that despite its pervasive poverty, the African continent represents an example of hospitality and generosity, is not shared by all observers. Thus, Gaim Kibreab asks: "African traditional hospitality, myth or reality?"

He attacks the belief, held by most writers on African refugee problems and international agencies, that refugees are generally welcomed by their co-ethnics across the border and that they are received with traditional hospitality and provided with the necessary means to earn their living. While Kibreab does not deny that this hospitality once existed, he says that in twentieth-century Africa it is a thing of the past.

> There is a catalogue in evidence which shows that African refugees are not always given a welcome emanating from "tribal" tradition, but are at times subjected to harassment, exploitation etc., and when they received a warm welcome it was mainly due to the advantages the local population hoped to enjoy as a result of such an influence. (1985, 68)

Acceptance of refugees worked as long as there were ample resources but, with droughts, warfare, and mass displacements, they have been severely depleted, leading Kibreab to conclude that "hospitality in a state of poverty is inconceivable." In Africa refugees might be treated better than in other places, but most nations do not have the necessary resources to maintain the ancient degree of hospitality that worked, says Kibreab, like this:

> The underlying logic of the so-called African tradition of hospitality is that because African ethnic groups are arbitrarily separated by borders that are not of their own making, the refugees' "co-ethnics" on the other side of the border not only receive them warmly, but will provide them with food, shelter and production inputs—land and other implements—so that after a certain period, the refugees attain the same

material level as their hosts. These refugees are believed to settle among their relatives harmoniously and are allowed to share the resources of the community. (1985, 69)

However, the vast majority of people are very poor, and while they may wish to assist the refugees, they do not have enough resources to do so. Therefore, Africa is no longer what it once was. According to Kibreab:

> These countries and especially their rural areas are characterized by an abject poverty and no matter how generous rural people attempt to be they have nothing more to offer but their hospitality—and hospitality in a state of wretchedness is like an electric lamp without electricity and a myth, to say the least. (1985, 69)

The author then proceeds with country-by-country examination and emphasizes repeatedly that many refugees become a source of cheap labour, and that in some countries they are accepted not on the grounds of hospitality but primarily because of economic advantages to the host nation.[7] He says that "On top of being impoverished they [the refugees who arrive] are politically vulnerable and this political vulnerability certainly makes them an easy prey to ruthless exploitation at the hands of the rich rural Africans" (1985, 80).

Disturbing trends, as the following list shows, were developing in Africa in the 1980s:

- In 1982, Djibouti forcibly repatriated a number of refugees back to Ethiopia.
- Throughout 1983 and 1984 Zambia intermittently repatriated refugees from Angola, Zimbabwe and Malawi with force.
- Nigeria expelled several thousand Ghanaians in 1983 as well as in 1985.
- In 1982 Uganda sanctioned military attacks on Rwandan refugees who had been resettled over twenty years in Uganda.
- Despite Tanzania's otherwise exemplary treatment of refugees over two decades, in late 1983 Tanzanian and Kenyan officials arrested and exchanged "dissidents," including a number of documented refugees.
- In February 1985, Tanzania and Uganda agreed that 10,000 ethnic Rwandans, expelled from Uganda in December 1983, would be repatriated even if force were necessary.[8]

Kibreab perceives a growing xenophobic attitude in many African states and notes that the number of forced expulsions represents a trend. "Mounting economic pressures and political instability in countries with sizable populations are easily explicable through scapegoating these 'alien' elements. Refugees can then become prey in a cynical game" (1985, 80).

Settlement Versus Integration

In a later study, Kibreab (1989) describes the different ways of treating refugees. The term "local settlement," he says, is often misunderstood. Scholars and international agencies, as he points out, tend to use local settlement and local integration synonymously. But in Africa local settlement means placement of refugees in segregated sites where their material needs (except land contributed by host countries) are met by the international refugee support systems. Therefore, "local settlements in the eyes of African host populations, host governments and refugees do not represent a solution. They are seen as temporary sites where refugees are provided with assistance by the refugee support systems to become self-supporting until the circumstances that prompted them to flee cease to exist."

"Integration" takes a different route. In Western nations, it represents an economic, social and cultural process by which refugees become members of the host society on a permanent basis, irrespective of how things develop in their countries of origin. This is followed by legal integration whereby the former refugees acquire the citizenship of the country of their asylum through naturalization.

The situation in Africa bears its own stamp. Thus the *Asylum Act* in the Sudan, which reputedly is among the most generous in the continent, states: "No refugee ... shall depart from any place of residence specified for him. The penalty for contravening this sub-section shall be imprisonment for not more than one year (*Asylum Act* 1974, Article 9 (2))" (Kibreab 1989, 471).

The former Sudanese Commissioner for Refugees argues against integration and makes clear that if it is to be considered a sort of naturalization, it is "completely rejected in the Sudan." He argues also that the refugees themselves will not like it.

> Being a refugee in a country for 20, 30 or 100 years, I don't think will deprive you of your own nationality, your own origin ... that is why

in Sudan you hear that refugees had adopted this policy of local settlement, rather than local integration.[9]

In the same manner Tanzania, also considered generous, discourages integration.

The government does not encourage spontaneous integration and there are fewer "free livers" outside refugee settlements than in any of the other host countries. Several ... settlements are so constituted as to prevent rather than further integration, freedom of movement has been curtailed in all settlements.[10]

The situation in Africa does in fact bear a stamp of its own:

The total refugee population in the continent is hosted by only 11 countries and these are almost all adversely affected by severe economic and environmental conditions ... Many of the countries of asylum are in the grip of economic crisis and they have consistently failed to deliver the essential goods and services to their own citizens, let alone to accept hundreds of thousands of refugees for integration in their societies ... Talk about integration is wishful thinking based on inadequate understanding of the economic, social and political realities of present day Africa. (Kibreab 1989, 474)

On the other hand, the UNHCR and other support agencies have approached the problem from the perspective of integration and permanence—apparently quite in contrast to the perception by both the host countries and the refugees themselves, who consider the problem as transient.

Another complication arises from the fact that refugees in settlements located in border areas become embroiled in the political struggles in their former homeland. They may favour the side which is opposed by the government of their present host nation. Refugee settlements are frequently moved inland so that their political impact becomes less apparent. Asfaha Shoa (1988) observed that settlements of this kind suffer from severe economic and political pressures, and their permanence and purpose are perceived differently by international aid agencies, the host nation and the refugees themselves.

All of this renders a confused picture that does not allow for easy generalizations.

A Positive Summary

Contradicting many critics, a former protection officer for the UNHCR in Africa, summed up his experience, and in doing so confirmed that, in 1989 at least, the traditions of African hospitality and humane treatment continued:

> It is first of all this tradition, often but not always helped by boundary-crossing, ethnic kinship, which has led to the safety of millions of refugees. Even apart from the consequences for the troubled econo-mies of the African continent, this should be considered as a major achievement in the field of human rights ... The degree of hospitality seems to vary with the quality of interstate relations, bad relations increasing the chance to attain asylum. More specially, friendship and extradition treaties can seriously frustrate the granting of asylum, whether or not the person concerned meets the refugee criteria ... It is hoped that the worsening economic situation in recent years in many African states will not compromise their traditional hospitality. (Westerflier 1989, 178)

Further support for this view was provided by the then head of the UNHCR, Poul Hartling (Denmark). He applauded African hospitality, noting that Africans had not asked that their refugees be settled on another continent, but instead were seeking to accommodate them.[11]

Similarly, the former president of Tanzania, Julius Nyerere, said that refugees of Africa are primarily an African problem, and an African responsibility.

When all is told, in Africa, borders are not fences and walls as they are in the West. This difference in approach to refugees is worthy of careful note.

Notes

1. See *International Legal Instruments on Refugees in Africa* (1979).
2. Ibid., 352ff.
3. Based on William A. Shack and Elliot P. Skinner (1979). See also the exhaustive analysis by Ogenga Ottunu (1994) in respect to the Sudan.
4. Shack and Skinner, 1979 [p. 125].
5. Italics in the original. For a history of the OAU's concern with refugee issues and the regulations pertaining to them, see C. J. Bakwesegha, in Adelman and Sorenson (1993), 6ff.
6. See the detailed table in Otunnu (1994), 8.
7. Kibreab (1985) makes specific reference to Angolan refugees in Zaire in this regard, 78.
8. From *Africa Today* 32, no. 4, 75.

9. Kibreab (1989), 472, quoting Attiya Mussa.

10. Ibid., quoting L. Holborn (1975).

11. Miller (1982, 21). The latest comprehensive treatment is provided in Adelman and Sorenson (forthcoming).

10

Four Asian Lands

Iran

Among the human leftovers of the Gulf War of 1991 were the refugees who fled from Iraq and were accommodated partly in Turkey but mostly in Iran, where a million of them arrived in the span of a few days. These refugees were Kurds and Shi'a Muslims.

However, a good deal of world attention was focused on refugees who had fled to Turkey, where the displaced were languishing under miserable conditions in mountain areas, enduring bitter cold, rain and lack of any decent facilities. Turkey's problem with its own Kurdish population, who agitated for independent status, caused the government to turn a cold shoulder towards these new Kurdish arrivals.

This contribution of Iran, which received many more refugees, was largely overlooked by the West, for the nation was isolated as a political leper. Yet, it behaved generously in this instance and was publicly acknowledged for doing so by the (NGO) U.S. Committee for Refugees, when it published *Mass Exodus—Iraqi Refugees in Iran* (1991). This account emphasized that the refugees were not only given ready access to the country but were also supported primarily by Iranian funds, since international support was lagging badly.

> In every city and town in which we traveled, we saw collection points for donations from the Iranian people. Even among the refugees who voiced complaints, expressions of gratitude toward the people and government of Iran were nearly universal. But many of the refugees asked us when international assistance would begin to appear ... the Iranian authorities have had virtually no contact with international agencies.[1]
>
> At the peak of the refugee influx, Iran hosted the largest refugee population in the world, some 4.16 million. The sudden arrival of Gulf War refugees came on top of the 2.35 million who were there after

having fled from Afghanistan, plus the large numbers who had taken
flight during the Iran/Iraq war and those who had left home when
Iraq invaded Kuwait.[2]

Yet, despite this enormous accommodation, Iran received a mini-
mum of credit or outside assistance. The United States, for instance,
contributed over $200 million to refugees displaced by the Iraqis, but
only 10 percent of this went to those who had chosen Iran.

These figures were compiled in 1991 and are therefore not up to date,
but their thrust is clear: just as refugee acceptance is dictated all too
often by political considerations, so is relief—even when it does not
require accommodating the refugees in person. The United States
simply looked away. Iran was not on its support list for countries
accepting refugees, and was not worth a positive comment. Politics
overrode acknowledgement of the decent behaviour of a nation that
had to be painted as evil incarnate and had therefore, by definition, no
mitigating qualities.

Cynics will say that, far from deserving accolades for moral action,
Iran was merely enacting policies that reflected its long-standing enmity with Iraq. As the United States had readily accommodated Soviet
refugees during the Cold War, so too did Iran accept refugees from its
arch-rival to the south. Morality was not the issue at all.

Certainly sentiments of this sort have their role in human events, but
such arguments in the end deny all morality and paint it as a mask for
something else. Cynicism has its role in politics, but it does not account
for everything.

India

For the most of its existence, India's record in refugee matters has been
very good, even though the nation never became a signatory to the UN
Convention. (On July 27, 1992, India did sign a memorandum of
understanding with the UNHCR.) According to Milton Israel:

> Despite the communal violence and religious chauvinism that informs
> contemporary Indian society, the Hindu tradition is an extraordinar-
> ily tolerant one. While India's population is 85 percent Hindu, it is also
> one of the four largest Muslim countries in the world. Its 14 major
> languages and more than 400 dialects reflect regional and ethnic
> identities that are homes within homes—the parts of an extraordinary
> synthetic culture. India has little to learn from the West about multi-
> culturalism.[3]

Forced repatriation of Sri Lankans, which was a consequence of the assassination of Prime Minister Rajiv Gandhi in May 1991, did, however, mar the Indian record. Suspicion fell on the Sri Lankan refugees in India of whom there were some 200,000 at the time. They were Tamil migrants and refugees who for roughly forty years had been engaged in a battle for the right to self-determination with the Sri Lankan government in Colombo. They took refuge in the Indian state of Tamil Nadu, where most were housed in special camps. When the repatriation order was promulgated, the camps closed. But only a portion of the refugees agreed to go home.

This order to repatriate represented, as indicated, a departure from previous Indian policy and was strengthened by the insistence of the Sri Lankan government, which predicted that unless all recent refugees were repatriated, the agitation of Tamil exiles in India would result in disrupting neighbourly relations.

In mid-1993, the situation was still fluid, but it needs to be noted that even now the universally accepted policy of nonrefoulement is not universally adhered to. The exception, in this case, is provided by the world's most populous democracy.[4]

On the other hand, India's willingness to provide refuge is apparent from the fact that 100,000 Tibetans have been at home in India since the Chinese invasion in 1950. In Milton Israel's words, "India offered hospitality to the Dalai Lama and many of his people at considerable political as well as economic cost. Relations with China continue to be affected by this decision."

Looking at another of India's relationships, the tensions between it and Pakistan represent a classic case of differential treatment of persons fleeing from the same country to the same host nation.[5] The devastating fight between Hindus and Muslims and the creation of Pakistan caused the displacement of some 14 million people between 1947 and 1951, and the death of 600,000. In 1950, the Nehru/Liaquat Pact provided that the "two governments agree to protect people who moved between the two countries as a result of communal violence, i.e., along religious lines, until the end of the year."

However, Hindus and Muslims who left East Pakistan for India were treated very differently. Hindus had no problem crossing the border and obtaining relief: they were treated as refugees. Muslims, on the other hand, had to dodge border patrols in order to avoid rejection and deportation, or they bribed their way to obtaining identification papers.

Even so, religious problems within India were less about the tensions between Hindus and Muslims, and had more to do with actual and potential conflict between Hindus and Sikhs. That tension led to increased emigration of Sikhs to Europe and the Americas; it has its special stamp both in that Sikhs (somewhat like Jews) consider themselves a people as well as a religion, and there is strong agitation from them for the creation of Khalistan, a separate Sikh state in what is currently the Punjab.

A final note is needed on another aspect of the impact of religion on Indian society. Hindu fundamentalists (if they may be so characterized) want to end India's tradition of secularism and want their nation to be recognized as a Hindu state. Yet, as Armatya Sen (1993) has pointed out, while pluralism remains an internal characteristic of Hinduism, the latest revisionist interpretation of Indian history downplays the contributions Muslims and other non-Hindus have made to the nation. There is little doubt, however, that the impact of neighbouring Iran and Pakistan, which have declared themselves Muslim societies, is reflected among an element of India's Hindus. At present, these trends have not scored a major impact, but they have disturbed the traditional religious and ethnic landscape.

Pakistan

The separation of East Pakistan from Pakistan and the formation of Bangladesh, caused violent conflict and created 9 million refugees between March and December 1971.[6] These refugees received different kinds of treatment: the majority were Bengali Hindus and were encouraged to go home, but 300,000 Bihari Muslims had no place to go and were treated poorly by Bengalis who considered them foreigners. They were Muslims and wanted to go to Pakistan, but only 110,000 were admitted in 1974; the rest continue to live in camps in a land they do not consider their home.

In 1983, a UN study declared Afghan refugees in Pakistan the world's largest refugee population.[7] In 1993, of 6.5 million remaining refugees, 3.5 were found in Pakistan, and the other 3 million, in Iran.[8] Ten years later, most were still refugees and millions were housed in about 330 camp-like villages situated in the two provinces of Baluchistan and North West Frontier, both of which border on Afghanistan.[9]

There is little question that the Pakistanis showed a remarkable degree of willingness to take in these refugees. Whence this readiness?

Doubtless the fact that the refugees were Muslims fleeing from a communist regime played a role. Another, and perhaps even more compelling factor, was the position Pakistan occupied in the East/West power struggle during those years. It was closely bound to the United States, which was supplying arms to the Afghan resistance fighters and channelling them through Pakistan. At the same time the United States provided Pakistan with arms and loans, and saw to it that the Afghan refugees received ready help from the UNHCR.

Cynics may therefore claim that once again, self-interest and not altruism was the main engine that drove Pakistan to accept masses of refugees. Still, even if Pakistan did hope that the refugees would eventually go back to their homeland, and did think that meanwhile it would be militarily and economically strengthened by doing the bidding of the United States and even if that was its dominant motivation, one would be forced nevertheless to conclude that this readiness to accommodate the Afghans was an instance of humane action paying handsome dividends. Either way the Pakistanis are to be commended.[10]

Japanese Perspectives

Japan was not only a latecomer to international relations (in 1853), but also a somewhat hesitant participant in refugee rescue and accommodation.

In 1974, the first Vietnamese refugees were received in Japan with sympathy. By 1981, 5,387 "boat people" had been admitted and granted temporary landing permission, but when many of the claimants were found to be of Chinese origin, refugee accommodation became muddled (Yasuhiki 1990, 84ff.). Between these two dates lie efforts by the Japanese government to square the traditional isolationism of the Japanese with international responsibilities. In the late 1980s, the country was represented at UNHCR executive meetings, and in 1981 it signed the UN Convention relating to the status of refugees. Because Japan faced considerable difficulties in attempting to integrate its own laws with those required by the Refugee Convention, it passed a new Immigration Control and Refugee Recognition Act in 1982. Currently, all refugees—regardless of the country in which the ships which brought them are registered—are allowed entry into Japan when refugee claimants are aboard.

Although there remains a tradition of excluding foreigners, the Japanese have supplied a large amount of money to the UNHCR and have played an active role in various refugee programs. They agreed to take in ten thousand Indochinese refugees, but this quota has not been filled to date. The reason is not necessarily Japanese foot dragging, but may be traced in part to the boat people themselves who, having found integration difficult in Japan, have prefered to go either to the United States or to European countries. Also, despite its generous financial support for international refugee resettlement, there have been problems over admitting people into the country. At one point the Minister of Foreign Affairs reportedly favoured opening the doors more widely, while the Minister of Justice did not wish to, saying that the UNHCR criteria ran counter to the tradition of national homogeneity and therefore were not "relevant to the Japanese situation" (Yasuhiki 1990, 86).

The reason for the shortfall was also influenced—so some critics say—by the Japanese practice of evaluating newcomers in terms of economic opportunities. While this charge appears to be based on the stereotyping of a whole nation and its traditions, it is nonetheless a fact that there was continued resistance by Japan to assume the kinds of responsibilities that, for instance, European nations assumed vis-à-vis Bosnian refugees, or that North American countries took on in accepting a large contingent of the fleeing Indochinese.

To be sure, Japan's extraordinary economic success has attracted many migrants and refugees from eastern and Southeast Asia. In 1990, some one hundred thousand non-Japanese Asians were working illegally in the country. Saito Yasuhiki (1990) speculates that Japan will be forced to deal with foreign workers—whether they are refugees or not—before the end of the century, and that it will need to open its borders to even larger numbers of migrants.

Western refugee authorities generally consider Japan at least ten years behind the trends found elsewhere, but this could be explained by the continuing tension in the country between traditional isolation on the one hand and a sense of international responsibility on the other. Mizuno Takaaki (1990, 89–93) describes this tension as "the refugee quandary":

> The influx of refugee boats also directed attention to the inadequacy of Japan's refugee policy. It raised the important question under what conditions Japanese society should open its doors to foreigners ... Public sympathy for the refugees and, more important, international pressure worked together to facilitate the welcome extended then— and now—to Indochinese refugees. In contrast, Japan has been tradi-

tionally unsympathetic to political refugees from other areas of the world. Only a small number of these people trickle into Japan, and they do not have the economic ties to Japan that Indochinese refugees do.

Still, Takaaki calls the acceptance of the Indochinese "noteworthy," for it marked a breakthrough in the traditional reluctance to accept outsiders into Japanese society altogether. Despite its adherence to the UN Convention, Japan's legal system makes it virtually impossible for refugees outside the Indochinese realm to be admitted. For instance, testimony by an individual to the effect that he or she is a refugee is not allowed and instead, concrete evidence is demanded—and usually not obtainable. Meanwhile, the adjudication process takes a long time, the refugee's visa usually expires before a decision is reached, and an appeal must be directed to the very person who has turned down his refugee status, namely, the Minister of Justice. Thus, thousands of Iranians and Afghans who applied for refugee status were generally refused admission and forced to look to Australia as a haven.

According to Takaaki in this same article,

> These issues have never been widely discussed in Japan, partly because Japanese have a preconceived image of refugees. In Japanese, the word *nanmin* (refugee) brings to mind war-scarred, starving people, and Japanese tend to forget the original meaning of the word— a person who flees for refuge or safety because of persecution.

Thus, while the Japanese readily support refugee work financially in overseas locations, they are not as quick to accommodate in Japan proper the needs that the enormous pressure of refugee movements has unleashed. As Takaaki notes, "Refugee aid drives in Japan have raised millions of yen in good-will contributions, but xenophobic locals repeatedly oppose the opening of refugee resettlement centres in their neighborhoods."

The reluctance of Japan to join in providing asylum was first linked to the fact that in the 1970s, the arrival of Chinese economic migrants posing as Vietnamese refugees led to a spate of media reports criticizing the government for being lax, and warning that refugees would destroy the country. Lately, however, there has been some loosening of exclusionary practices, and the fact that thousands of non-Japanese now live in the country for commercial and other reasons has created some acceptance of foreigners. There is still little acceptance of refugees though, because, for the most part, they are not seen as contributors to the economic infrastructure. But, says Takaaki (1990, 93),

Japan, which has until now unquestioningly defined itself as a homo-geneous society, may be on the brink of having to accept a new self-image as a society composed of people of diverse origins. It can foster that image by acknowledging the beacon of hope that it is for refugees and laborers alike—and acting accordingly.

Notes

1. *Issue Brief*, July 1991, 6–7.
2. In 1993, some three million Afghan refugees were still in the country; see U.S. Committee for Refugees (1993), *World Refugee Survey*, 90–91.
3. Milton Israel, in correspondence with the author, August 1993.
4. For details, see Asha Hans (1993).
5. For further treatment, see Aristide Zolberg and others (1989).
6. For a view from the Indian perspective, see Sahai (1948); see also Elbright (1954).
7. "Sustaining Afghan Refugees in Pakistan," (1983); see also the follow-up report, "Afghan Refugees in Pakistan: From Emergency to Self-Reliance" (1984).
8. U.S. Committee for Refugees (1993), *World Refugee Survey*. 90–91.
9. For more recent figures, see U.S. Committee for Refugees (1993), *World Refugee Survey*.
10. For a brief history of the Soviet invasion of Afghanistan and the conse-quent refugee problem, see U.S. Committee for Refugees, *Afghan Refugees in Pakistan: Will they go home again?* (1982).

11

Glimpses of Europe and Central America

Germany[1]

Currently, 6.3 million foreigners live in Germany alongside about 78 million Germans. Nearly half of the foreigners arrived in the 1960s and 1970s as contract labourers from Turkey, Yugoslavia, Italy and Greece. Also residing in the country are 20,000 Vietnamese, Mozambican and Cuban nationals, who had gone to work in what was then East Germany. During the last few years, Germany has experienced an enormous influx of refugees—in 1991 there were 256,112; in 1990, 193,630; and in 1992, 438,191. In early 1993, additional hundreds of thousands of refugees arrived from Eastern Europe, especially from the former Yugoslavia, Romania and Bulgaria.

In 1992, 2,285 acts of rightist violence occurred there, most of them against foreigners or their homes. Seventeen people were killed in these attacks. Cornelia Schmalz-Jacobsen, Germany's Federal Commissioner for Immigrant Affairs, commenting on the ensuing public revulsion, said, "Our society and our political leaders have shown that this violence is something we do not want in our country. We can't say the problem is behind us, but we can breathe a sigh of relief."

The relief, however, proved to be premature. While in the first ten weeks of 1993 the number of incidents was down significantly, about 50 percent from the comparable period in 1992, it rose again in subsequent months and immigrants were again being killed and their homes torched.

The government of Chancellor Helmut Kohl, with the agreement of the major opposition parties, decided to placate widespread unhappiness with the constitutionally demanded generous refugee policy by amending the constitution radically. In early March 1993, the German Bundestag debated these amendments. *The Week in Germany* reported on March 5:

The new laws will [also] affect ethnic Germans and foreign workers in Germany, but are primarily intended to reduce the number of foreigners who enter the country to claim asylum. The new legislation is based on the assumption that the large majority do not have a valid claim to asylum under the provisions of article 16, the constitutional article that guarantees asylum for the politically persecuted. Such persons, who are believed to come to Germany because they seek a better life, not because they face political persecution in their countries of origin, would no longer be able to apply for asylum.

While there was a general agreement by the major parties on the outline of the new legislation, disagreements arose over details. Opposition also came from Amnesty International, and demonstrations against the introduction of the law took place in a variety of cities. At issue was the virtual abolition of a basic principle that a political refugee had a right to asylum. ProAsyl, a national organization opposing the amendment, said that Article 16 had set a new standard for refugee protection, and its abolition or mutilation would weaken trust in the new Germany.

Meanwhile, German legislators were contemplating easing the process by which foreigners who were legitimate residents of the country could apply for naturalization. German citizenship laws were and are still highly restrictive. Even children born in Germany are not eligible if their parents aren't citizens, though according to official figures foreigners generate nearly one-tenth of Germany's gross national product. One out of every four workers in the steel industry is foreign-born, as are 20 percent of hotel workers. But the emphasis here was once again on "racial purity," and the old and infamous *jus sanguinis* (law of blood relations) was evoked:

Persons who have German blood, be it however diluted, are German. Foreigners, on the other hand, remain foreigners, unless they go through a complicated process of naturalization that is not possible until after 15 years of residence and requires relinquishing the original citizenship. The policy means that ethnic Germans whose tie to Germany is often quite tenuous, are entitled to immediate German citizenship, while Turkish guest workers remain foreigners over generations. Immigrant nations such as the United States follow *jus soli*, the law of the soil. Those born on United States soil to foreign parents are U.S citizens.[2]

There was widespread feeling in Germany that current restrictions smacked too much of racial concepts and not enough of humanitarianism. Consequently, the country's Federal Commissioner for Immigrant Affairs supported the granting of naturalization after eight years and called for the introduction of dual citizenship. She submitted draft legislation to this effect and also proposed adoption of the American system, by which to children born in Germany would have automatic citizenship.

After vigorous public debate and demonstrations pro and con, the law was amended on July 1, 1993. Among its contents were a loosening of naturalization procedures and a list of "safe countries" (were persecution is presumed not to exist or which are presumed to have proper refugee determination systems). On it are most of the nations of Eastern Europe, as well as India, Ghana and Senegal. In addition, persons who enter Germany from states that are members of the European Community or other neighbouring countries are excluded from applying for asylum. Among them are Austria, Switzerland, Poland and the Czech Republic. In effect, by declaring all nations that are neighbours of Germany to be "safe" countries, immigration and police officers are able to turn back arrivals at the border without a hearing.

But, as the amendment was taking effect, antiforeigner excesses continued:

> Attacks on foreigners have increased sharply in Germany in the two months following passage of a strict anti-asylum law that was partly intended to stop the wave of violence. Statistics from two federal agencies that track the violence showed that the number of burnings, stabbings and beatings inspired by neo-Nazi sentiment increased following the May 28 passage of the law by Germany's parliament. The day after the law was passed, young radicals bombed a house in Solingen, in northern Germany, killing five Turks. Neo-Nazis launched 76 additional firebombings in June, compared to 33 in May. According to the office for the protection of the constitution, about 1,180 serious right-wing-motivated crimes were recorded this year through July 22, compared to 788 in the same period of 1992.[3]

In January 1993, a poll showed that about 37 percent of all German citizens endorsed the epithet *"Ausländer raus!"* (Foreigners out!). An even larger number averred that "Germans had to defend themselves in their own country against foreigners."[4] It must be noted, however, that despite all the attention on such sentiments and the violent attacks on "non-Germans," there were other voices defending the need for both immigration and a humane treatment of refugees.

Thus, a prominent publishing house issued a paperback by journalist Roland Tichy (1990), tellingly entitled *Ausländer rein* ("Foreigners in," instead of "out"). In it, he made six proposals

1. German nationalism and racism must not rise again;
2. We must arrive at a humane way of speaking about foreigners;
3. Naturalization must be made easier;
4. Germany was and is a land of immigration;
5. Immigration must have some limitations; and
6. Foreigners must be treated like other Germans and be acknowledged as such.

In sum, the violence perpetrated against strangers has altered the landscape of German refugee policy. Before Article 16 was amended it was a beacon of hope; today it flickers but dimly. Still, enough Germans want to do better: they have kept alive the flame of compassion and have made the moral dilemma in refugee protection a continuing national issue.

The European Community

James Hathaway warns that the impending creation of the European Community may mean that refugees will be kept out of Europe altogether. Individual nations, already worried that their identity is being submerged in the new Europe, are worried that their own immigration and refugee barriers will be supplanted by a much less secure frontier— that of "Fortress Europe." Such an eventuality, many believe, will threaten the cultural homogeneity that has been the characteristic of even the smallest countries. Therefore, great pressure has been exerted on the nascent European Community to create strict criteria for the admission of foreigners. According to Hathaway,

> This consensus is devastating for refugees. Governments have decided to treat migrants from the less developed world as an undifferentiated evil: refugees, economic migrants, drug traffickers and terrorists are officially categorized as presenting a unified threat and will all confront a common policy of deterrence. This response to the alleged menace of "foreigners" effectively buries any concern for the human rights principles of international refugee law. (1993b, 15)

The way in which the European Community expects to handle immigrant and refugee pressure is to impose visa requirements on nationals whose countries habitually produce migrants and refugees,

combined with a heavy penalty against carriers that bring undocumented persons to the continent.

> Only citizens of states that accept this obligation to block the entry of
> "undesirable" national groups will be granted unrestricted freedom of
> movement within Europe. Those European states which have tradi-
> tionally allowed foreigners to make their case for admission at a
> domestic point of entry are in effect being required to choose between
> continuing that policy and extending unrestricted regional freedom of
> movement to their nationals.[5] (Hathaway 1993b)

Central America

Mexico was receptive to the Spanish Republican refugees of Franco's
time, and acted generously towards some Spanish-speaking refugees
like Chileans and Uruguayans. Yet other refugees, such as those from
Guatemala or El Salvador, were held at bay because, while their cultural
affinity would qualify them for a show of generosity, their political
activities, it was feared, would create political instability in Mexico
itself.[6]

Still, in 1989 Mexico had 300,000 to 400,000 Central Americans in its
territory. Most, though, were only on their way elsewhere, especially to
the United States. In addition, 40,000 Guatemalan peasants and 5,000
Salvadorans in Mexico were recognized by the UNHCR as refugees, but
not by Mexico, which saw them rather as temporary asylees. Thus, in
the summer of 1981, when 2,000 Guatemalans arrived in Mexico, the
government deported them forthwith, because they did not meet what
were said to have been the individual requirements for asylum. However, the real reason lay elsewhere: Guatemala wanted its refugees back
and Mexico complied, fearing that Guatemala would extend its warfare
into Mexico (Zolberg 1989, 215).

The uneven treatment of the Guatemalans in Mexico is analyzed by
Zinzer (1991, 62):

> For the most, those Guatemalans who left their country as an ethnic
> and linguistic group and preserved their social cohesion in Mexico
> gained the status of refugees. On the other hand, refugees who fled
> into areas of Mexico other than the state of Chiapas and scattered in
> search of jobs rather than establish refugee camps, were denied official
> refugee status. The major factor in acquiring refugee status was
> residence in an official camp.

Mexico was attractive to Salvadorans and Guatemalans for a number of reasons: its cultural affinity, political stability, better economic conditions, social support networks, earlier migrations of family or friends to Mexico and, last but not least, its accessibility.[7] The irony is, of course, that Mexicans themselves migrate in large numbers to the United States, legally and frequently illegally, not for political but for economic reasons.

Thus, Mexico becomes a paradigm for global migrations: refugees arrive in large numbers and, when given the opportunity, will supplant the lowest economic stratum of the new country, while the weakest economic elements of the receiving nation find their own position untenable and seek economic asylum elsewhere. Central American refugees arrive in Mexico, and Mexican workers leave for the United States. The paradigm is underscored by the fact that Mexico does not recognize Central American migrants as political refugees but considers them, as it does its own emigrating population, economic migrants.

In July 1990, the Mexican government yielded to international and national pressure and incorporated a new category of a refugee into its legal definition. A refugee was now defined as someone who,

> to protect his life, security, or freedom, threatened by generalized violence, foreign aggression, internal conflict, massive violation of human rights, or other circumstances that have seriously disturbed public order in his country of origin, is forced to flee to another country.

In Mexico church and state have been and are in conflict with each other over the interpretation and application of refugee legislation. The latter has acted to protect political considerations, the former to obey a moral injunction. The dioceses of San Christobal, Tapachula, and Cuernavaca were especially prominent in involving the church in refugee assistance, which was carried out without government involvement and even before the government had decided what to do about the refugees.

It should be noted that Mexico has not become a signatory to the UN refugee conventions, and it was not until after prolonged negotiations in 1982 that the UNHCR was allowed into the country.

Zinzer holds that the general Mexican policy, even though it has on other occasions exhibited humanitarian purposes, has—with regard to Guatemala—treated refugees in the context of its own political interests. Refugees were assigned to camps and could not leave without permission, as there was widespread fear that they might take over rich tropical areas of Chiapas or that they would so contaminate the political environment that social tensions in Mexico would rise, especially in poor areas.

All these illustrate that political and economic refugees are increasingly intermingled. The old definitions are crumbling and new realities are urgently demanding their reconsideration and reframing.

The politics of refugee movement is also demonstrated in the way Honduras has conducted its affairs: refugees from Nicaragua were tolerated during the '80s because the Honduran government sympathized with their cause, while Salvadoran refugees were restricted and harassed because the Honduran government thought that they were economic migrants, ideologically undesirable, and/or guerrilla supporters.

In addition, the United States has had much influence on Honduran policy, and the civilian population of Honduras, unlike that of Mexico, showed little support for refugees. When the government bowed to international pressure to help the displaced, Salvadorans were put into isolated settlements, which some observers characterized as virtual concentration camps and which the U.S. State Department euphemistically called "closed camps under the protection of the armed forces." In contrast, Nicaraguan refugees were given preferential treatment because they fit the general military and political objectives of the U.S. government, and the Honduran government adjusted its refugee policy accordingly.

Thus, Central America provides an example of the kind of refugee treatment in which the moral, humanitarian or religious impulse that fuels refugee acceptance is strongly mixed with and overpowered by political considerations.

This intermingling is highlighted also by the location of the refugee camps. The Roman Catholic Church, which fosters a humanitarian approach to refugee movements, wants these camps close to Honduras's border with El Salvador, because this makes it easier for refugees to flee to Honduras and, conversely, for refugees to return to their home country. On the other hand, the United States has urged the Hondurans to move the camps away from the border to reduce the possibility of their serving as bases for guerrillas fleeing from pursuit by the Salvadoran army. Honduras itself wanted to repatriate the refugees when the conditions in El Salvador improved, but the Salvadoran government paid no attention to the Honduran attempt (Rosenberg and Shepherd 1986, 205).

Costa Rica is unique—in the Americas and in most of the world. While it borders on two states with long military pasts (Nicaragua and Panama), it has no army and uses the large expenses saved thereby for education and social services. It is a stable country with a sound democratic tradition.[8]

It also has a humanitarian reputation, having provided asylum to refugees who fled from Chile, Argentina and other South American countries during the days of their totalitarian governments. Thus, at the beginning of 1979, Costa Rica—which itself has a population of only about a million and a half—accommodated 50,000 fleeing Nicaraguans. But, a half year later, when the Somoza government was overthrown and replaced by the Sandinistas, most of the refugees returned to their homeland.

A few years later, Costa Rica again received refugees, from El Salvador, Cuba, Guatemala and, in minor numbers, from other Central and South American countries. In 1986, Costa Rica housed about 30,000 refugees, and the estimate at the time was that, in addition, over 200,000 illegal foreigners were in the country. As of December 1992, 32,350 refugees were recognized; 80,000 more were undocumented, most of these came from Nicaragua.[9]

These pressures began to have their impact on the traditional sense of Costa Rican fairness and openness, and caused a shift in its policies favouring restriction over acceptance.

Notes

1. On the communitarian implications of Germany's refugee acceptance, see Chapter 7 above.

2. *This Week in Germany*, March 5, 1993.

3. *The Globe and Mail*, July 31, 1993.

4. *Das Parlament*, Bonn, 8/15, January 1993, 1.

5. See also E. Whitaker (1992), 193.

6. Wipfler (1985), 114. See also World Refugee Survey: *Country Report on Mexico* (1993).

7. By the end of 1991, most Salvadoran refugees in Mexico had been repatriated.

8. The following analysis is based on Basok (1988).

9. World Refugee Survey: *Country Report on Costa Rica* (1993), 143.

12

The North American Experience

U.S. Perceptions and Policies

For the greater part of its existence, the United States has considered itself as the land to which the dispossessed of the earth could come and find refuge. Already in 1776 Thomas Paine predicted that America would become the world's "land of asylum."

Engraved on the Statue of Liberty's pedestal is Emma Lazarus's poem, which proclaims:

Give me your tired, your poor,
Your huddled masses yearning to breathe free,
The wretched refuse of your teeming shore.
Send these, the homeless, tempest-tossed to me—
I lift my lamp beside the golden door.

The first major restrictions on what had been virtually unhindered and universal admission were directed a hundred years ago at Orientals and were followed after World War I by the introduction of quota systems regulating the flow of immigration.

The United States signed the Geneva Convention in 1951 and in the course of years instituted an elaborate system of refugee regulations. There were sporadic admissions of special groups of refugees, such as Hungarians and Czechs who had resisted Soviet oppression, and the boat people who were fleeing from disturbances in Southeast Asia. But otherwise, refugees were accorded individual consideration, in accordance with the Convention and U.S. law, administered by the Immigration and Naturalization Service (INS).

But that system encountered two problems. First, the United States was so desirable that immigrants as well as refugees often used illegal means of getting to it and staying there; and second, the very extent of its borders and shores made watertight control impossible.

In addition, the United States like any other country, had conflicting ideals and politics, with the latter more and more frequently gaining the upper hand. Thus, refugees from Nicaragua, which had a Communist government, were accepted, while Salvadorans fleeing their nation's regime were for many years not considered refugees because the American government supported the country's regime. But, in 1990, new regulations improved the 1980 Refugee Act, and accorded Salvadorans Temporary Protected Status (TPS), which provided that after eighteen months their cases would be reviewed and a determination would be made as to whether returning to their homeland was now safe. This was not so much a divergence in principle (the 1980 Act had already stipulated a one-year TPS for refugees), as a recognition that El Salvador had indeed been a refugee-producing country—an assumption hitherto denied.

TPS constituted an important extension of the Geneva Convention. It temporarily protected aliens designated by the Attorney General as having been forced to flee their homelands because of ongoing armed conflict, environmental disaster, or other extraordinary and temporary conditions. TPS for Salvadorans expired in mid-1992 when civil strife ceased and refugees began to return in larger numbers. But, since El Salvador was unable to accept so many returnees at once, the United States granted them Deferred Enforced Departure (DED), which allowed them to work and stay for the time being. Nationals of Kuwait, Lebanon, Liberia, Somalia and Bosnia-Herzegovina were also eligible for TPS. In the judgement of Bill Frelick (1992), Senior Policy Analyst for the U.S. Committee for Refugees, U.S. policy has lately been less influenced by ideology and politics, and Salvadorans have gained permanent refugee status by and large at the same rate as Haitians and Guatemalans (28, 30 and 21 percent, respectively).[1]

There is no question that the insistent appeal of religious and other refugee support groups for fair and equitable treatment has had an effect on U.S. policy, and that it has is an important reminder that democracy may in the end yield to demands for legal consistency, if not always to moral imperatives. In the United States, this has been particularly so in the case of Haitian refugees.

The Haitian Challenge

The latest Haitian crisis erupted after President Jean-Bertrand Aristide was ousted in September 1991 by a coup d'état and tens of thousands of Haitians fled the island for fear of reprisal by the military junta. The United States resolved to prevent their arrival on U.S. soil because once there they would be able to present their claim to refugee status—a process that would last for years. President George Bush issued an Executive Order, by which the U.S. Coast Guard would interdict all ships likely to have refugees on board. INS officials would then interview passengers and screen them to determine whether they would be allowed to enter the United States or be returned to their homeland. In 1991, no fewer than 40,000 Haitians were sent back.

Ambassador Brunson McKinley defended the policy, saying, "The perception that we are treating Haitians differently than asylum seekers from other nations ... is not true. In fact, we are admitting to the United States large numbers of Haitian asylum seekers."[2]

This is not the place to argue the legitimacy of this procedure, which was strongly opposed by the UNHCR. But, despite the criticism, the American administration became even more restrictive and took to sending boats back without officers conducting any interviews at all.[3]

President Bill Clinton promised in his election campaign to reverse this harsh treatment of Haitians, but has, since reaching the White House, reversed himself and continued the Bush policy.[4]

Civil rights and refugee advocates wonder not only about the legality of this whole procedure, but also about whether it would have been undertaken if these boat people had been Europeans, that is to say, whether racial prejudice did not play a role in this sordid business. Whatever the answer, it is unclear whether President Clinton had honestly intended to follow certain moral guidelines in this matter, and—as in the matter of assuring gays and lesbians equality in the armed forces—pulled back because practical politics seemed to demand a course that candidate Clinton had flatly declared immoral.

The odious policy has little to recommend it. The Haitians have been kept at bay, but their inability to land and claim refugee status has robbed America not only of daring, self-reliant people, but also of credibility in matters of refugee protection. Neither the Geneva Convention nor the U.S. Immigration Act foresaw such interdiction, and the Statue of Liberty seems tarnished in the process. So many of the tired and poor were not allowed to pass.[5] On the front cover of a prestigious historical journal, the Statue assumed a very different pose: instead of lifting a lamp, it pointed its finger away from the United States.[6] The Haitian crisis demonstrated that often morality has to stand back before considerations that have little to do with the plight of refugees and everything with the raw bones of politics.

A key judicial case that resulted from this affair was *Haitian Refugee Center v. Baker*.[7] In it, the legality of halting refugee boats in international waters and returning them to Haiti was challenged. The Court of Appeals instructed the lower court to dismiss the argument, and the U.S. Supreme Court declined to hear the case.

Associate Justice Harry A. Blackmun was the only dissenter. He felt that the case was of real significance and should have been heard. If indeed the Haitians were to be returned to an uncertain future in their strife-torn homeland, that ruling, he believed, should come from the Supreme Court after careful consideration of the merits of their claims. But the highest court did not hear the case, and Bill Frelick commented gloomily on its dismissal: "It could mean the end of asylum as we know it."[8]

Yet there are times when the old religious and moral urge which most Americans profess becomes visible and produces unforeseen results. The movement to harbour refugees from the pursuit of the INS was a significant force in the sanctuary movement of the 1980s. There are voices today that call for its resuscitation (see Chapter 3).

Response in Canada

The late 1970s was the time of the Indochinese "boat people." Media reports showed them roaming aimlessly at sea, and these pictures had a strong moral impact on Canadian citizens.

Professor Howard Adelman, fueled by his own strong convictions, formed Operation Lifeline and was successful in awakening Canadian awareness of the Indochinese tragedy. Media coverage produced a groundswell of public outrage, which moved the government to open its borders, and in 1979 and 1980 the nation took in 60,000 of the refugees.

To be sure, approval for this influx was far from unanimous; still, the government for once followed the strong urging of a united religious community (Adelman 1982, 1–3). The spring of 1979 saw many religious groups becoming sponsors of refugees, and this private sponsorship vastly increased not only their numbers but also put pressure on the government to sponsor more refugees itself.

Operation Lifeline had two major moral roots. One was clearly church/synagogue oriented; the other stemmed from a generalized sense of social obligation, which found a particular echo in the tradition of the New Democratic Party. Jews especially were touched by the images that flashed across their television screens. They remembered 1939 when the steamship *St. Louis* was roaming the sea with 907 desperate German Jews on board. They had set sail from Hamburg to seek refuge somewhere. They had entry visas for Havana, but on arriving in Cuba they were turned back.

> The search for a haven now began in earnest. Argentina, Uruguay, Paraguay and Panama were approached, in vain, by various Jewish organizations. Within two days all the countries of Latin America had rejected entreaties to allow these Jews to land, and on June 2nd the *St. Louis* was forced to leave Havana harbour. Their last hope was Canada or the United States, and the latter, not even bothering to reply to an appeal, sent a gun boat to shadow the ship as it made its way north. The American Coast Guard had been ordered to make certain that the *St. Louis* stayed far enough off shore so that it could not be run aground nor any of its frantic passengers attempt to swim ashore. (Abella and Troper 1982, 63ff.)

This was the famous "voyage of the damned," which made few headlines at the time but became, in retrospect, a symbol of how refugees were treated during that period.[9]

Canada's then Prime Minister, Mackenzie King, and his chief lieutenant in the immigration service, Frederick Blair, were thoroughly unsympathetic, and so the *St. Louis* headed back to Europe where many of the passengers eventually died in the gas chambers of the Third Reich.[10]

The movement championing the boat people of 1979 brought about an outburst of public humanitarianism and social activism and in this respect it was similar to the sanctuary movement in the United States.[11]

Although on the whole, the churches were more interested in Latin American refugees than in those coming from Southeast Asia, they nonetheless played a highly significant role in Operation Lifeline.[12]

Twelve years later the problem of the boat people was still alive, but conditions in many of the Western countries, especially Canada, had changed significantly. Other refugees demanded attention, and the countries of first asylum in Southeast Asia, especially Hong Kong, bore the brunt of the problem. There was a growing feeling that this part of the world dealt with economic migrants rather than conventional refugees, and this gave Western nations an opportunity to close the book on the Vietnamese boat people, at least for the time being.[13]

.While up to the mid-1980s Canada's policies were refugee-oriented,[14] with worsening economic conditions they became increasingly restrictive. A new Immigration Act was passed; appeals were limited; a "third safe country" clause was instituted (though not applied at once); and refugees once again became headline news. But the signals were somewhat mixed.[15]

Gender Bias as a Refugee Claim

On January 16, 1993, *The Globe and Mail* reported the following:

> Canada has no intention of leading an international campaign to accept persecution based on a person's sex as sufficient ground for refugee status, Immigration Minister Bernard Valcourt said yesterday.
>
> Mr. Valcourt suggested that widening the Geneva Convention definition of a refugee to include sex as a basis for refugee status would open the flood gates to women fleeing abuse at a time when Canada is trying to control the refugee flow.

The case that caused these comments concerned a Saudi Arabian woman called Nada, who had claimed refugee status in 1991 and averred that she had been stoned and beaten for refusing to wear a veil, and for objecting to laws that discriminate against women. Canada's Immigration and Refugee Board denied her claim to refugee status, on the ground that Canada's law and the Geneva Convention do not include gender bias in their definitions. In addition, the Board added its own highly dubious advice and counselled the woman to comply with Saudi Arabian laws instead of criticizing them.

Valcourt approached the problem from yet another angle, in declaring why Canada would not intervene:

> Will Canada act as an imperialist country and impose its values on other countries around the world? I think this is a legitimate issue that we should discuss, but I don't think that Canada should unilaterally try to impose its values on other countries regarding laws of general application.

This argument seems to put the entire issue of refugee determination on its head. For what is the Geneva Convention but a moral judgement of offending countries' policies? Any time that a nation accepts a person as a legitimate refugee it is judging the refugee's country of origin. In issuing his high-sounding observation, the immigration minister merely used terms like "imperialist" to evade a serious issue. However, he eventually did allow Nada to remain in Canada. James Hathaway finds that this particular ruling does not portend a widening of the refugee definition. In fact, he says, singling out gender alone for privileged consideration would be unjust to other pressing needs:

> The problem is that if one, at this stage, pursues the inclusion of gender and leaves aside all of these other important categories [like family, sexual orientation and social class] that are seen to be without the social-group category, I think you end up privileging one form of disenfranchisement over all the others.
>
> If we were to reopen it [the refugee definition] in the age of restrictionism in which we live, there is an overwhelming probability that a lot of the protections that refugees currently enjoy would be taken out of the Convention. There is a big risk factor if you are going to reopen an international convention in an era when Canada is the best player on a bad team.[16]

Public interest had recently focused on Ferdousi Bhuyian, a twenty-year-old native of Bangladesh whose marriage had been arranged when she was eleven, and who had been beaten almost to death by her husband. In February of 1993 authorities had ordered her deportation and she had since been in hiding in Montreal in a shelter for battered women. Her fate was eased when in early 1993, new guidelines were issued by the Immigration and Refugee Board (IRB) according to which women who can prove that they are fleeing from domestic violence in their country of origin would be recognized as refugees.

> The guidelines advise the members of the Immigration and Refugee Board how to deal with cases in which women say that they were victims of discrimination or persecution because of oppressive laws, sexual violence, religious precepts, or other reasons.
>
> For example, the panels are required to assess whether "state authorities inflict, condone, or tolerate violence, including sexual or domestic violence." They are also required to consider the difficulties that many women may suffer when they testify about sexual violence in public.[17]

A month after the above guidelines were put into effect, a Canadian court further expanded protection for refugees.

> The court was overturning a refugee panel's decision to deny refugee status to Ting Ting Cheung and her six year old daughter Karen Lee who had entered Canada in 1989. Mrs. Cheung had violated China's one-child-per-family law by having a second child, and faced compulsory sterilization, she said.

> The court decided that it wouldn't offer judgment of China's one-child policy, but said implementing that policy by forced sterilization is a form of persecution because it violates Canadian and international standards of human rights.
>
> There is a point at which cruel treatment becomes persecution regardless of whether it is sanctioned by law. Forced sterilization of women is so intrusive as to be beyond that point ...[18]

The Immigration and Refugee Board panel had said that China's one-child policy was not intended to persecute women, and was "simply the implementation of a law" that applied to everyone and not to the claimant in particular. The court, in rejecting this view, said that if a law's *effect* is to persecute it does not matter what its *intent* might be. Even laws that apply generally may persecute if they are implemented in a brutal way, and a woman who has had a child and any of her children born later may be considered to be a group that needs protection from persecution.

Some refugee advocates criticize the new guidelines for not including "gender" as a separate category of persecution. For example, Leanne MacMillan (1993, 3) comments:

> The guidelines do not create a separate category of persecution labelled as "gender," and do not separately categorize gender as one of the five grounds upon which to found a refugee claim ... The proposition put forward in the guidelines is, in one instance, that the claimant must show an individual persecutory foundation to her claim, and, in another instance, it would seem that a situation of generalized oppression of and violence against women will not be a ground for a claim to be rejected ... it is difficult to know when an individual basis for the fear of persecution need be shown and when it need not.

Since the release of the guidelines, the IRB has identified about 350 gender-related claims in one year.

The debate about gender discrimination as a ground for seeking refugee status has not yet been resolved. It looms as an important new moral issue.

New Canadian Realities

Changes to the Immigration Act that took effect on February 1, 1993, have been hotly debated. Many of its provisions (like the "safe country" clause) had been opposed by the Canadian Council for Refugees and its constituent organizations. Subsequently the government arranged for an immigration consultation in various parts of the country. Obviously, the results of these consultations were not binding on the government, but they did point to emerging trends (Immigration Canada 1993). What they reveal is a widespread emphasis on moral responsibility for the major issues of refugee policy.

In the government's summation of these discussions, it had the following to say about Convention refugees:

> A number of participants, particularly in Toronto, thought that the government interpretation of the Convention definition of a refugee is too narrow, and hope to see the definition applied more generously in the future. They pointed to apparent discrepancies between the way the definition is interpreted by visa officers and the way it is interpreted by most non-governmental organizations. They felt the need for greater communication and information sharing on this issue between field officers, NGOs, and church groups.

On the matter of gender persecution, it said

> Many participants emphasized that Canada can and should offer refugee status to women who are fleeing harsh treatment in their home countries as a result of their gender. Many thought that such women should be included within the definition of "refugee" in Canadian legislation, and that Canada should lobby the UN for appropriate changes in the Convention definition ... There was clear agreement that women fleeing repression because of their gender should be assisted, whether the Convention definition applied or not. (Immigration Canada 1993, 15)

All told, Canada had not shut its gates as was feared, not yet anyway. Refugee advocates continued to lobby for a policy that would reflect a strong moral commitment.[19]

Notes

1. But see his pessimistic assessment after the Supreme Court ruling on the Haitian boat people, further on.

2. "U.S. Policy", *Refugees* (Geneva), September 1992, 36.

3. For details, consult Frelick (1992b), 153 ff., and Osuna and Hanson (1993), 42 ff.

4. In April/May 1994, President Clinton introduced procedures with regard to Haitians that were more lenient.

5. Between September 1991 and June 1992, some ten thousand Haitians were in fact admitted, but more than double that number were turned away. At

the same time over 130,000 refugees were admitted from the former Soviet Union and from Vietnam.

6. *American Heritage,* February–March 1994.

7. James Baker was Secretary of the State under President George Bush. Regarding this case, he was executing President Ronald Reagan's Executive Order 12323, under which the Coast Guard could turn away any vessel when there was reason to believe that an offence was being committed against United States immigration laws "provided that no person who is a refugee will be returned without his consent." The plaintiffs based their case on this last provision.

8. *Refugees,* September 1992, 37.

9. See Thomas and Witts, *The Voyage of the Damned* (1974).

10. It was Blair who, when asked how many Jews should or could be admitted to Canada, answered "None is too many."

11. Adelman (1982), 88–89. Adelman calls Bernice Gerrard (a leader in the movement) an "activist alderwoman with a strong Christian conscience," and speaks of the then Mayor of Ottawa, Marion Dewar, as being "motivated, in part, by a strong social conscience, with roots steeped in the NDP's tradition of social activism."

12. Detailed information on the contribution of various religious groups may be found in Adelman (1982), 112ff.

13. According to Lawrence Lam (*Refuge,* 13, no. 5), 100,000 Southeast Asian refugees were still languishing in camps and detention centres in the Philippines, Indonesia, Hong Kong, Malaysia and Thailand.

14. In fact, they merited a special commendation by the UN.

15. For a recent overview of refugees in Canada, see the special edition of *Refuge* 13, no. 9.

16. *The Globe and Mail,* Feb. 5, 1993.

17. *The Globe and Mail,* March 10, 1993.

18. *The Globe and Mail,* April 3, 1993.

19. Since this chapter was written, the new Liberal government commissioned a review of IRB policies; the resulting report is now under consideration.

13

The Sanctuary Movement

Roots

The word *sanctuary* is a translation of the Hebrew *miqdash*, meaning a holy place. It was applied to the Tent or Tabernacle, and here the first test of "sanctuary" in the modern sense is recorded.

Upon Solomon's accession to the throne (tenth century B.C.E.), Joab, who had been the general of King David's army, knew that his days were numbered, because he had killed his predecessor, Abner. Consequently, the Bible records (I Kings 2:28ff):

> He [Joab] fled to the Tent of the Lord and grasped the horns of the altar ... King Solomon was told that Joab had fled to the Temple of the Lord and that he was there by the altar; so Solomon sent Benaiah, saying: "Go and strike him down." Benaiah went to the Tent of the Lord and said to him [Joab], "Thus said the King: Come out!" "No!" he replied; "I will die here." Benaiah reported back to the king that Joab had answered him thus and thus ...

It so happened that Solomon disregarded what had been an old custom, namely, that "grasping the horns of the altar" guaranteed at least temporary asylum, and despite its disregard by Solomon the custom persisted.[1]

In the eighth century B.C.E., a member of the royal household of the Kingdom of Israel by the name of Isaiah ben Amoz had a great many unusual ideas about the politics of his country. His sayings had an enormous influence on Judaism and subsequently on a nascent Christianity, and as late as this century had an effect on refugee protection.

At that time, there were disturbances in Moab, which lay to the east of the Jordan River, and apparently the turbulence caused many people to flee the land. Neighbouring Israel was one of the places to which they fled, despite the traditional enmity which had existed for some centuries between the two nations. The fugitives reached the Arnon River, which at that time served as the border.

It seems that the question arose: What shall we do with these Moabites who are not wanted in their own country and whom—as Moabites—we don't want either?

Isaiah described them as "fugitive birds, like nestlings driven away," and in God's name he advised his country's ruler and citizens:

> Conceal the outcasts, betray not the fugitives.
> Let Moab's outcasts find asylum among you;
> Be a shelter for them against the despoiler.[2]

We have no record how Isaiah's message was received in his day, but we do know that the spirit which animated it had a profound influence in our own time.

The Sanctuary Movement in the United States

In Judaism, Christianity and Islam, religion and state should ideally have a relationship that would benefit both to the utmost. The more orthodox the citizen, the more likely he/she will give religion a position of dominance; while liberals are wary of such close ties and would keep religion and state apart as far as possible. Religion, they would say, should function through voluntary adherence of the believers, without the state's support or interference.

But even in the United States, where the separation of church and state has become a kind of "religion" of its own, the sacred was never totally divorced from the profane. Christmas is a statutory holiday, and in many states certain Sunday restrictions on public activities still obtain. Congress begins its sessions with an opening prayer; chaplains serve in the armed forces and are paid by the federal government. Even in time of war, persons are exempted from military service if they can demonstrate that their religious conviction prohibits them from serving; and theological students of all denominations were exempt from the draft in World War II. The battle over abortion is unabashedly based on religious conviction by the Pro-Life forces; and proposals for legalized euthanasia have received a similar reception from all mainstream religious groups. Censorship is based in part on secular and in part on religious considerations; and a child given out for adoption will usually be placed in a home professing the same religion as the natural mother or father.

While the majority of the Founding Fathers were declared deists, many of the modern presidents of the United States have been professing theists and active members of their church. One recent president, Jimmy Carter, was a "born-again Christian," that is to say, one having close links to the evangelical position.

The sanctuary movement of the 1980s therefore struck a highly responsive chord in the American mind. Jim Corbett, a Quaker rancher, played a large role in spreading the sanctuary gospel.[3] At the same time, the religious community in universities was energized by William Sloane Coffin, who was a chaplain at Yale University before he became senior minister of the prestigious Riverside Church in New York. Corbett, Coffin and their associates began to protect undocumented aliens—refugees and migrants—on their church premises and gave them sanctuary.

By 1983, there were 45 public sanctuary sites in the United States, with 600 congregations and religious organizations supporting the movement. A year later the number had grown to 150, and these primarily sheltered Central American refugees. In retrospect, the sanctuary movement was unique for the way it involved religious groups in American politics. While opponents of liberalized American immigration have advanced a great variety of reasons for their position, those responsible for the sanctuary movement were overwhelmingly motivated by their religious convictions, though some probably catered to the religious bent of many people in order to win them over politically.

Morality and Law

From the very beginning, the movement's practitioners set their religious beliefs against the dictates of federal statutes that made it a crime to knowingly conceal or harbour any alien not lawfully entitled to enter or reside in the United States.

One of the more fascinating aspects of the movement was the way in which some of its practitioners viewed the relationship between their actions and a federal law that made their activities criminal. Some saw the law as immoral, and believed that their religion demanded that they resist the state's immorality. Civil disobedience was therefore considered a religiously sanctioned action.

Others saw the tensions somewhat differently. They found the law not only immoral but also illegal in that it contravened America's obligations under the Geneva Convention. Civil disobedience was therefore not the issue: resisting such a law was legal.

Tom Gerety (1988, 163ff.) analyzed the differences between the two best-known practitioners and theorists of the movement, Jim Corbett and William Sloane Coffin. According to Gerety, Corbett was

> an innocent [who stumbled] upon a wrong [El Salvadorans fleeing their country and being stopped by U.S. officials at the border] that a less generous soul would have ignored. The innocent attempts at what seems a straightforward, unthreatening, gesture of amelioration. Then he himself is wronged. This leads to anger and so to further involvement and further acquaintance with the wrong. Hesitation gives way to commitment. Soon the protagonist has found the cause, an all-consuming commitment to righting a set of wrongs.

In contrast, Coffin had always been an activist, he was church connected and had his church behind him; and he did not, like Corbett, need to be converted to the movement. For him, it was a natural, progressive actualization of his faith.

Thus the unknown rancher and the well-known pastor were involved in a remarkable enterprise, though they had different ideas of how their movement could be most effective. Coffin had political know-how and wanted to utilize the proper channels by which one could put pressure on the government, so that the laws regarding refugees could be changed and Salvadoran and Guatemalan refugees could stay in the United States until it was safe for them to go back home. Meanwhile, churches, synagogues and all people motivated by religious impulses should do their utmost to have Congress and the President change a bad law.

Corbett, on the other hand, brought a less sophisticated and essentially crusading religious spirit to the movement. He was less enamoured of the normal processes, believing them too slow and sometimes unavailing. In Gerety's words,

> Sanctuary is the needle's eye through which congregations composed of the beneficiaries of violence are entering into active community with the violated ... the church in sanctuary begins at last to free itself from seventeen centuries of ... violence, exploitation, and persecution. This makes the Nuremberg Principles of non-cooperation with crimes against humanity the basis for understanding the legal status of sanctuary efforts.

In this classic conflict between morality and law, the sanctuary adherents tried to establish a new basis for justifying their actions. Their secular arguments averred that U.S. refugee policies discriminated against those fleeing oppression at the hands of governments supported by the United States.

For others, religious precedents were more important than legal procedures. In addition to the above-noted instances from the Hebrew Bible, they drew on examples from the ancient Greek tradition of sanctuary for escaped slaves and other fugitives, early Christian legislation by both Emperors and Popes who permitted churches to grant asylum to fugitives, and a range of examples from English legal history in which monasteries, churches, and even towns for centuries enjoyed the power to shelter fugitives from blood feuds as well as from persecution by the king.

This tradition gave rise both to the vocabulary of sanctuary in English and to the arguments that churches should enjoy genuine legal immunity and not just immunity from intrusive search and seizure.

The sanctuary movement also pointed to the function of international law, such as the Refugee Convention. Though in the United States it has not assumed the status of federal law, it demands adherence, and theoretically the entire refugee practice of the Immigration and Naturalization Service is based upon it. In the end no one can enforce conventions and international laws unless the Security Council of the United Nations takes it upon itself to do so.

But when religious impulse and secular law come in conflict, the religious impulse becomes translated into a moral law, so that two laws stand opposed to one another and each person must decide which should be obeyed. The apparently obsessive trend in the sanctuary movement to look for a legal construct that would validate its practices stems directly from this. Religious conviction evokes religious law and the state lays down secular law. If the latter is proven to be faulty or immoral, it must give way to the higher and more perfect law.

Ignatius Bau (1985) has given us some statistics on the results of this conflict. Sanctuary workers were on a number of occasions hauled into court but invariably received very light and often suspended sentences. One of the high profile cases occurred in 1984 when Jack Elder, a sanctuary worker, was arrested, charged and indicted by a federal grand jury on three counts of transporting undocumented aliens. It was the first time that the federal statute was invoked, and it was also the first time that the government "invaded" church property and made the arrest—thereby violating the very idea of sanctuary. It is worth noting that Elder was acquitted on a legal nicety, a result which satisfied neither side: the prosecution was unhappy because it had failed in a landmark case; the sanctuary movement, because the trial did not invalidate the state's transgression of the ancient sanctuary precept.

Later on, Elder was charged again and found guilty on six counts. He received six one-year prison terms, which were to run concurrently, but the sentence was later changed to 150 days in a halfway house.

In 1985, the U.S. government announced that sixteen more workers had been indicted, and during the year the count of arrests went up. Personal residences of some of the sanctuary workers were broken into and searched; relevant evidence was seized, but at a trial in Phoenix and another in Tucson, the sixteen who had been indicted and had pleaded not guilty were released, despite the fact that a number of them— although they had promised not to violate any laws as part of their release—announced that they would continue their work. Here, the construct that the sanctuary movement had created made it possible for them to promise faithfully to observe the law and not to consider a violation of the federal statutes as "breaking the law."

In sum, it can be said that the sanctuary movement won its immediate battle with the state, but it did not win the war. The refugee law is still in existence and Central Americans still suffer discrimination. Of late the movement has received little publicity, but it could be assumed that under proper circumstances it would again come to life. Whatever its future, one thing is clear: its very existence brightened the refugee scene during the 1980s and made it clear to the world that refugee protection could derive enormous strength from moral considerations. Canada and Great Britain also experienced, to some extent, the impact of the movement.

A New Canadian Movement

In the summer of 1993, an "Ontario Sanctuary Coalition" spearheaded an appeal to the Minister of Public Security, who under new regulations was put in charge of immigration and refugee matters. At issue was the impending deportation of twenty-two refugees and their families who were about to be returned to their countries of origin.

A letter to supporters stated:

> As you know, we have promised to provide Sanctuary should our government fail to act with justice and mercy. We hope for the sake of the refugees that we will not have to take this drastic step. We ask for your prayers for a speedy and positive resolution.

The idea behind this latest effort to protect refugees was launched in the spring of 1992 as a "civil initiative" (rather than an exercise in civil disobedience)—an idea Jim Corbett had put forward. The Canadian government was seen as breaking its international commitments, and therefore law-abiding, religiously motivated persons felt it was their responsibility to protect the unprotected. While the churches would not themselves hide the refugees—people would be hidden in the community—they would be the spiritual spearheads for moving the Canadian public to a level of ethical awareness. There would be no repetition of the situation that the Jews of Germany experienced in the 1930s, when everyone looked away while they were being deported to their deaths.

In an address to the Canadian Council for Refugees, Mary Jo Leddy (1993)[4] traced the reconstituted sanctuary movement in Canada and outlined its objectives.

> Our struggle to protect innocent refugees whose lives are at stake is also our struggle to reaffirm the heart and soul of the decency that is Canada. In a time where many preach a politics of despair and division, we have acted on the belief that we have been, we are, much better than this ...
>
> Our involvement as a coalition began in a very small way in June of 1992. Refugees began showing up in the early mornings and late evenings at the offices and homes of various advocacy groups. The claims of these refugees had been refused by the Immigration and Refugee Board (IRB) and their appeals to the Federal Court had been rejected. They had received deportation orders.
>
> These refugees came to Amnesty International, VIGIL and Romero House ...[5] We knew that some of [the refugees that came to us] had their legitimate claims refused because of negligent lawyers, incompetent translators or clearly biased board members—over half of the cases we were concerned about had been heard by members of the IRB and had been dismissed or disciplined because of their conduct during the period of these refugees' hearings...
>
> Initially, we pursued all the avenues that had been open. We wrote and spoke to the office of the Minister of Immigration with all the evidence in hand. We were told that all such decisions had been delegated to local Immigration officers. When we went to local Immigration officers we were told that there was nothing that could be done without the Minister's permission. The system seemed in gridlock, shock-proof.
>
> Finally, we were faced with people who were to be deported—whom we knew to be in extreme danger. In a dialogue with them, it was decided that the only option was for them to go into hiding. During the summer of 1992 we arranged for a protective situation for

two families with five children each, and two for single men. They were "hidden" by religious communities and ecumenical groups in Ontario. This meant that their room and board and living expenses were provided by church groups throughout the Province. The Canadian Autoworkers provided some money for their living expenses. Doctors and hospitals volunteered their medical services. Schools accepted to educate the children—in full knowledge of their situation. These refugees were in safe keeping because of the decency of so many people.

The speaker did not mention her own involvement, but she was the prime mover who, along with journalist June Callwood, succeeded in getting attention from the media as well as from the highest levels of government. They ended this campaign by calling for an independant public inquiry into immigration in Canada, claiming that critical documents, which spelled life and death for refugees, were either lost, destroyed or distorted. As to why this had happened, they said, "Only an inquiry can answer this question."

> We believe that such an inquiry is not only in the public interest, it is also in the interest of those empolyees of Immigration Canada who are attempting to act honestly and fairly.
>
> However, we feel an obligation to say this clearly: until such a review happens, we all must admit that any Post-Claim Review at Immigration Canada is a farce. It is a make-work, make-money project for the employees of Immigration Canada. (Leddy 1993)

Leddy justified the revitalization of the sanctuary movement by pointing out that during the last year no requests for a humanitarian and compassionate review had been granted in Ontario, and called it "useless for refugees" to pay the required $450 to have their case reviewed. Speaking with great passion, Leddy ended by saying that it was time to stop playing "bit parts in this made-in Ottawa soap opera that has no happy endings."

Romero House in Toronto became the focus of the new Canadian movement. However, the movement's beginning came at a time when the majority of Canadians had begun to feel that there were too many immigrants and refugees arriving in the country.[6]

Notes

1. An ancient altar with horns was excavated in the 1970s; see *Biblical Archeology Review*, Vol. 1, no. 1 (1975), 1ff., which includes a picture. The

biblical scene was reenacted 2,200 years later when Thomas Becket was struck down at the altar by emissaries of Henry II of England. Meanwhile, however, religious places continued to enjoy protection from the state's intrusion; and as late as the nineteenth century, escaping American slaves could flee to churches and be granted asylum—even though by law their "owners" had a right to recapture them, and those who prevented their recapture were considered felons under federal law. This scenario may be considered an immediate predecessor to the sanctuary movement of the 1980s. Another source to which we have repeatedly referred comprises the passages in the biblical Book of Numbers (Chapter 35), where six cities, three west of the Jordan and three east of it, were set aside for persons fleeing from the blood avenger. They were entitled to asylum if they could show that they had slain another person without intent (Plaut (1981), 1249–50; Milgrom (1990), 504–8). For more examples of asylum, including diplomatic asylum, see Sinha (1971), 5ff.

2.   Isaiah 16:3–4.

3.   He and John Fife, an Arizona preacher, helped initiate the movement.

4.   See above, Chapter 3; she was speaking for the Ontario Sanctuary Coalition.

5.   The speaker had been a member of the Sisters of Sion and had moved into Romero House to share her life with the refugees residing there.

6.   *The Globe and Mail*, March 22, 1993. A further survey found 53 percent of a sample expressed that opinion, a sharp rise from previous attitudes.

14

A Final Look

Deficiencies in the Law

While the number of refugees in the world has increased, the willingness to help them has decreased, and existing laws have not been able to deal with increasing needs. According to Nanda (1989, 9), the major problems with refugee law may be summarized as follows:

1. It does not address the issues of people who do not fit the persecution standard of the Convention passed after World War II. Today they are fleeing more often because of serious internal instability, disturbances or armed conflict, and are unable or unwilling to return. It also does not deal with refugees stranded within their own country.

2. States grant ... asylum to those falling within the scope of the refugee definition, and since the nonrefoulement protection is applicable only to those ... who meet the persecution standard contained in the Convention definition, a large number of asylum seekers are denied the Convention protections.

3. The plight of a stateless refugee, who has no nationality, who has little or no protection, has not been addressed.

4. No Convention has addressed the question of resettlement.

5. The law has never dealt with mass expulsions.

International refugee law has additional deficiencies: it addresses only individuals who can prove that they fall within the text of the definition, but protects neither the individual who is a de facto refugee (though "merely" uprooted), nor the group that needs assistance. It deals with the principle of nonrefoulement, which provides that people are not to be sent back if they are refugees but says nothing about any right to asylum.

The general response to these problems has been to increase restrictions and to strengthen existing laws and institutions, rather than to develop a wider vision based on moral perceptions that international action needs to be taken to deal with the refugee problem. Law often acts as the mediator between morality and national self-interest; but if the latter is its sole master, it fails to fulfil this vital task.

The Moral Dimension

As one surveys the morality of refugee protection one sees a lamentable, though not entirely unexpected, discrepancy between the ideal and the actual. Refugees are usually sheltered more readily in poor countries than rich ones. Africa generally attempts to help its own refugees, and in Asia, Pakistan has taken much responsibility for Afghan refugees—developments that have put a serious strain on the already depleted resources of the countries that offer asylum.

In fact, it appears that richer countries will all too often disdain refugees from poorer countries, as if the resources which they create for their own consumption were being depleted by those who want a place at the trough. In consequence, some refugees are allowed entrance, but not so many that they will endanger the standard of living of the host nation.

The conundrum is further complicated by national politics. Accepting an individual refugee under the Convention appears to imply that his/her country of origin, by creating refugees on its territory, does not live up to proper international standards. But if that country is on good diplomatic terms with the one where refuge is being sought, a political dilemma frequently surfaces: the country of asylum does not wish to publicly judge the country of the refugees' origin. This was especially the problem with El Salvador and the United States, with the latter reluctant to take in the refugees of the former because close ties existed between them at the diplomatic level.[1]

While political refugees can still find asylum on an individual basis, their chances of being accepted as members of a group beset by natural misfortunes, wars and the like, grow constantly dimmer. The number of refugees is increasing the number of potential host countries is decreasing; and the richer the latter, the more restrictive they will be. Nowhere else is the question of the morality of refugee legislation more clearly highlighted than in this respect.

What is the future of those who are presently mired in countries that offer only temporary asylum? Theoretically, repatriation would be the preferred solution, but that rarely occurs, and will certainly not happen in the near future. Wars and revolutions seldom make it possible for refugees to opt for a quick return.

Local integration in the country of first asylum is a possibility, but very often—as in much of Africa—it is impeded by ethnic and tribal groupings and traditions. There may also be political strategies, by which refugees would be kept in their camps, in order to produce pressures on the country of origin.

Ultimately, resettlement is the only long-term solution, but the countries most capable of accommodating the refugees are on the whole the least willing to accept them. Considerations based on morality pale before those based on xenophobia, ethnic and religious preferences, as well as on national politics.

Refugee policy is often beset by an "all or nothing" propaganda: either you save all refugees or you save none. In practice, this amounts to a national loss of moral sensitivity, and while it is obvious that no nation can take all the refugees who will seek to join it, each has an obligation to save as many refugees as possible. Peter and Renata Singer (1988, 122) conclude that an equal consideration of interests is a basic moral principle, which is often ignored in refugee policy.

There are also short-term and long-term considerations. In the short term, it is true that refugees may (like regular immigrants) take jobs from the resident community, but generally speaking this is not the case. Newcomers most often take those jobs which resident workers refuse; anecdotal evidence supports this.

In the long term, most developed nations will benefit from immigration and especially from refugees, because the latter have displayed initiative and stamina in their escape from harsh conditions and represent a valuable resource that will benefit their adoptive country.

Taking up the lifeboat parable, Gary E. Rubin (1991, 64) reflected: "How do we answer our central question: 'Are there too many people in the lifeboat?' My answer is that there are slightly too few."

In his address to the spring consultation of the Canadian Council for Refugees in 1992, Guy Goodwin-Gill said:

> We are entering a new legislative era and that implies reformulating a number of questions: What is the aim of the protection? Is asylum the best solution for refugees? Why distort, through endless analysis, the

essentially humanitarian instrument of the Geneva Convention on the Status of Refugees? Is it useful to invest increasingly large sums in the determination of refugee status? It is not the question of persecution but of protection that must be at the core of the debate. The most recent UNHCR surveys show that in the world today, one person out of 135 is a refugee or a displaced person. It is not so much the number of refugees but the categories that tax the organization's instrumental protection. The task at hand is to redefine who should be protected by the international community in the context of present-day flows and circumstances. (1992, 1)

The religious and moral conditions of most nations speak of the need to make some sacrifices to help others. While on a one-to-one basis this is often demonstrated as the virtue of individual citizens, somehow on a national basis sacrifice gives way to comfort, and principle to politics. This is a human dilemma, and in the area of refugee policy where the odds are heavily stacked against one side and time is often of the essence, it comes into sharp focus and thus becomes a theme of our age.

Still, the moral impulse is not without resonance. It may motivate only the few who care, yet their conviction and persistence have on many occasions sensitized the national conscience and have moved governments towards a more generous refugee policy.

Notes

1.   See Chapter 12, and Singer and Singer (1988), 112–14.

Appendices

Appendix A:
Egyptian and Hittite Treaties[1]

Extradition of Refugees to Egypt

[If a great man flee from the land of Egypt and come to the Great Prince of Hatti] ... The Great Prince of Hatti shall cause them to be brought to Usermaat-Re Setep-Re, the great ruler of Egypt, their lord, [because] of it. Or if a man or two men—no matter who—flee ... they shall be brought to Ramses Meri-Amon, the great ruler of Egypt.

Extradition of Refugees to Hatti

Or if a great man flee from the land of Hatti and [come to User]-maat-[Re] Setep-en-Re, the [great] ruler of Egypt, or a town or a district or a ... belonging to the land of Hatti, and they come to Ramses Meri-Amon, the great ruler of Egypt, Ramses Meri-Amon, the great ruler of Egypt, shall cause them to be brought to the Prince [of Hatti] ... Similarly, if a man or two men—flee ... He shall cause them to be brought to the Great Prince of Hatti.

Extradition of Egyptians from Hatti

If a man flee from the land of Egypt—or two or three—and they come to the Great Prince of Hatti, ... they be brought back, ... to the great ruler of Egypt. But, as for the man who shall be brought to Ramses Meri-Anon ... do not cause that his crime be raised against him; do not cause that his house or his wives or his children be destroyed; [do not cause that] he be [slain]; do not cause that injury be done to his eyes, to his ears, to his mouth, or to his legs; do not let any [crime be raised] against him.

Extradition of Hittites from Egypt

Similarly, if men flee from the land of Hatti ... and they come to User-maat-Re Setep-en-Re, the great ruler of Egypt. ... they be brought to the Great Prince of Hatti ... the Great Prince of Hatti shall not raise their crime against them ...

Extradition of Fugitives

[If a nobleman flees from the Hatti land and if] one (such) man comes ... the great king, the king of the land of Egypt, in order to enter his services ... the great king, the king of the Hatti land, shall seize them and shall have them brought back to the king of the Hatti land.

[If a nobleman] flees [from Rea-mashesha] ... Amana, the king of the land of the Hatti land, shall seize him and shall have him brought to ... Amana, the great king, the king of Egypt, his brother.

If one man flees from the [Hatti land or] two men [or three men and come to] Rea-mashesha mai [Amana, the great king, the king of the land of Egypt], [Reamashesha] mai Amana, the great king, [the king of the land of Egypt, shall seize them and have them brought back to] Hattusilis, his brother ... hence [let them not *exact punishment for*] their sins, ... let them not *take revenge upon* their people ...

Dealings with Foreigners, *etcetera*

If anyone of the deportees ... removed escapes and comes to you ... you do not seize him and turn him back to the king of the Hatti land, and even tell him as follows: "Go! Where you are going to, I do not want to know," you act in disregard of your oath.

If a country or a fugitive takes to the road and while betaking themselves to the Hatti land pass through your territory, put them on the right way, show them the way to the Hatti land and speak friendly words to them! ... If you do not put them on the right way, (if) you do not guide them on the right way to the Hatti land, but direct them into the mountains or speak unfriendly words before them, you act in disregard of the oath.

Or if the king of the Hatti land is getting the better of a country and puts them to flight, and they come to your country, if then you desire to take anything from them, ask the king of the Hatti land for it! You shall not take it on your own! If you lay hand on it by yourself or conceal it, (you act in disregard of the oath).

Furthermore, if a fugitive comes to your country, seize him.

Appendix B:
Human Rights—Major Documents

It is instructive to read the major documents of modern times that deal with human rights and their origins. In some cases the latter are stated outright (as in the American Declaration of Independence) and in others they seem to derive from natural law.

The selection presented here is admittedly eclectic; it is meant to reflect the mainstream of thought that has been regnant in the industrial world for the last two centuries.

The Virginia Declaration of Rights

This document was adopted in Virginia on June 12, 1776.

> A declaration of rights, made by the Representatives of the good People of Virginia, assembled in full and free Convention, which rights do pertain to their posterity as the basis and foundation of government.
>
> I. That all men are by nature equally free and independent and have certain inherent rights, of which, when they enter into a state of society, they cannot by any compact deprive or divest their posterity; namely, the enjoyment of life and liberty, with a means of acquiring and possessing property, and pursuing and containing happiness and safety ...

The Declaration of Independence

Adopted by the Continental Congress of the United States on July 4, 1776, this document's language and spirit are similar to those of the Virginia declaration, which is not surprising since Thomas Jefferson was the chief author of both.

> When in the Course of human Events, it becomes necessary for one People to dissolve the Political Bonds which have connected them with another, and to assume among the Powers of the Earth, the separate and equal Station to which the Laws of Nature and of Nature's God entitles them, a

decent Respect to the Opinions of Mankind requires that they should declare the causes which impel them to the Separation.

We hold these truths to be self-evident, that all Men are created equal, that they are endowed by their Creator with certain unalienable Rights and among these are Life, Liberty and the pursuit of Happiness.

That to secure these rights, Governments are instituted among Men deriving their just Powers from the Consent of the Governed.

Declaration of the Rights of Man and of the Citizen

At the beginning of the French Revolution the Constituent Assembly adopted, on August 27, 1789, the Declaration of the Rights of Man and of the Citizen.

Article I proclaims that "men are born and remain free and equal in rights"—but six years later the Thermidorian Convention, ruled by conservative republicans and constitutional monarchists, phrased the declaration of rights differently and stated: "Equality consists in the fact that the law is the same for all" (Article III). Social and other more precise rights were no longer recognized.

The Universal Declaration of Human Rights

A series of international conventions were agreed to in the nineteenth and early twentieth centuries. It was not until after World War II, however, that human rights achieved a place of central attention. The war had been characterized by an unprecedented disregard for human dignity and decency, with the Holocaust being the prime but not the only example of degradation and slaughter. Shortly after the end of the war a newly formed United Nations adopted, on December 11, 1946, resolution 96 (I) which condemned genocide as a crime in international law. The movement towards an international standard of rights culminated with the Universal Declaration of Human Rights on December 10, 1948. Its second paragraph states in part:

All human beings are born free and equal in dignity and rights. They are endowed with reason and conscience and should act toward one another in a spirit of brotherhood. Everyone is entitled to all the rights

> and freedoms set forth in this Declaration, without distinction of any kind, such as race, colour, sex, language, religion, political or other opinion, national or social origin, property, birth or other status ...

Note that here, in contrast to the American Declaration of Independence, the origin of the rights is not specified as being a divinity, since the politics of Soviet Union prohibited its inclusion. But here also, for the first time, the rights of refugees are set forth in a general fashion: "Everyone has the right to seek and to enjoy in other countries asylum from persecution." It may be fairly stated that the Declaration thus grounds the rights of refugees, as an aspect of human rights in general, in some form of natural law, which is to say that the rights are assumed in their origin to be of such nature that they need not be specified or specifically acknowledged.

The Helsinki Agreement

The Helsinki agreement of August 1, 1975, which contained a ringing affirmation without a mechanism of promotion and enforcement, repeated the earlier declarations that human rights and freedoms "derived from the inherent dignity of the human person are essential for his free and full development."

Here, too, compromise was the order of the day, and with communist states as partners to the agreement, freedom of movement was singularly absent, as it could not be agreed upon.

The Canadian Charter

Finally in this catalogue, the Canadian Charter of Rights and Freedoms of 1982 should be mentioned. This document returns to acknowledging God as the source of rights, and begins by stating:

> Whereas Canada is founded upon principles that recognize the supremacy of God and the rule of law:
>
> *Guarantee of Rights and Freedoms*
>
> 1. *The Canadian Charter of Rights and Freedoms* guarantees the rights and freedoms set out in it subject only to such reasonable limits prescribed by law as can be demonstrably justified in a free and democratic society.
>
> *Fundamental Freedoms*
>
> 2. Everyone has the following fundamental freedoms:

a) freedom of conscience and religion;
b) freedom of thought, belief, opinion and expression, including freedom of the press and other media of communication;
c) freedom of peaceful assembly; and
d) freedom of association ...

Appendix C:
Refugee Documents

Convention Relating to the Status of Refugees
Done at Geneva on 28 July 1951

Preamble

The High Contracting Parties

Considering that the Charter of the United Nations and the Universal Declaration of Human Rights approved on 10 December 1948 by the General Assembly have affirmed the principle that human beings shall enjoy fundamental rights and freedoms without discrimination,

Considering that the United Nations has, on various occasions, manifested its profound concern for refugees and endeavored to assure refugees the widest possible exercise of these fundamental rights and freedoms,

Expressing the wish that all States, recognizing the social and humanitarian nature of the problem of refugees, will do everything within their power to prevent this problem from becoming a cause of tension between States ...

Chapter 1: General Provisions

Article 1: Definition of the term "Refugee"

A. For the purposes of the present Convention, the term "refugee" shall apply to any person who:

before 1 January 1951[2] and owing to well-founded fear of being persecuted for reasons of race, religion, nationality, membership of a particular social group or political opinion, is outside the country of his nationality and is unable or, owing to such fear, is unwilling to avail himself of the protection of that country; or who, not having a nationality and being outside the country of his former habitual residence as a result of such events, is unable or, owing to such fear, is unwilling to return to it.

Article 2: General obligations

Every refugee has duties to the country in which he finds himself, which require in particular that he conform to its laws and regulations as well as to measures taken for the maintenance of public order.

Article 3: Non-discrimination

The Contracting States shall apply the provisions of this Convention to refugees without discrimination as to race, religion, or country of origin.

Article 4: Religion

The Contracting States shall accord to refugees within their territories treatment at least as favourable as that accorded to their nationals with respect to freedom to practice their religion and freedoms as regards the religious education of their children.

Article 33: Prohibition of expulsion or return ("refoulement")

1. No Contracting State shall expel or return ("refouler") a refugee in any manner whatsoever to the frontiers of territories where his life or freedom would be threatened on account of his race, religion, nationality, membership of a particular social group or political opinion.
2. The benefit of the present provision may not, however, be claimed by a refugee whom there are reasonable grounds for regarding as a danger to the security of the country in which he is, or who, having been convicted by a final judgement or a particularly serious crime, constitutes a danger to the community of that country.

Article 34: Naturalization

The Contracting States shall as far as possible facilitate the assimilation and naturalization of refugees. They shall in particular make every effort to expedite naturalization proceedings and to reduce as far as possible the charges and costs of such proceedings.

Protocol Relating to the Status of Refugees of 31 January 1967

The States Parties to the present Protocol,

Considering that the Convention relating to the Status of Refugees done at Geneva on 28 July 1951 (hereinafter referred to as the Convention) covers only those persons who have become refugees as a result of events occurring before 1 January, 1951,

Considering that new refugee situations have arisen since the Convention was adopted and that the refugees concerned may therefore not fall within the scope of the Convention,

Considering that it is desirable that equal status should be enjoyed by all refugees covered by the definition in the Convention irrespective of the dateline 1 January 1951,

Have agreed as follows:

Article I: General provision

1. The States Parties to the present Protocol undertake to apply Articles 2 to 34 inclusive of the Convention to refugees as hereinafter defined.

2. For the purpose of the present Protocol, the term "refugee" shall, except as regards the application of paragraph 3 of this Article, mean any person within the definition of Article 1 of the Convention as if the words "As a result of events occurring before 1 January 1951 and ..." and the words "as a result of such events," in Article 1 A (2) were omitted.

3. The present Protocol shall be applied by the States Parties hereto without any geographic limitation.

Article II: Co-operation of the national authorities with the United Nations

1. The States Parties to the present Protocol undertake to co-operate with the Office of the United Nations High Commis-

sioner for Refugees, or any other agency of the United
Nations which may succeed it, in the exercise of its functions, and shall in particular facilitate its duty of supervising
the application of the provisions of the present Protocol.

2. In order to enable the Office of the High Commissioner, or
any other agency of the United Nations which may succeed
it, to make reports to the competent organs of the United
Nations, the States Parties to the present Protocol undertake
to provide them with the information and statistical data
requested, in the appropriate form, concerning:

   (*a*) The condition of refugees;

   (*b*) The implementation of the present Protocol;

   (*c*) Laws, regulations and decrees which are; or may
   hereafter be, in force relating to refugees.

Notes

1. Pritchard (1955), 200–205.
2. Date amended by the "Protocol Relating to the Status of Refugees of 31
   January 1967."

Bibliography

Abella, I., and H. Troper. 1982. *None Is Too Many*. Toronto: Lester and Orpen Dennys.

Adelman, Howard. 1969.*The Beds of Academe: A Study of the Relation of Student Residences and the University*. Toronto: Praxis Books.

———. 1982. *Canada and the Indochinese Refugees*. Regina: L.A. Weigl Educational Associates.

———. 1985. "Palestinian Refugees and the Peace Process." In *Peacemaking in the Middle East*, edited by Janice Gross Stein and Paul Marantz. London: Croom Helm.

———. 1988. "Palestinian Refugees: Economic Integration and Durable Solutions." In *Refugees in the Age of Total War*, edited by Anna Bramwell. London: Unwin Hyman.

———. 1991. "Refugees or Asylum: A Philosophical Perspective." In *Refuge or Asylum: A Choice for Canada*, edited by Howard Adelman and C. Michael Lanphier. Toronto: York Lanes Press Ltd.

———. 1992. Talk on Middle Eastern Refugees, September 30, York University.

———. Forthcoming. "Justice, Immigration and Refugees." In *Immigration and Refugee Policy: Australia and Canada Compared*, edited by Howard Adelman, Lois Foster, Alan Borowski and Meyer Burstein.

———. 1994. Forthcoming. Adelman, Howard, and John Sorenson, eds. *African Refugees*. Boulder: Westview Press and Toronto: York Lanes Press.

Adler, Stephen. 1980. "Swallow's Children—Emigration and Development in Algeria." In *Migration for Employment Project, World Employment Programme Research Working Papers, May 1980*. International Labour Organization.

Africa Today. 1985 (32, no. 4). "Africa Rights Monitor African Refugees: Patterns and Policy."

Ardrey, Robert. 1987. Contributor to Reynolds, Falger, and Vine, eds., *The Sociobiology of Ethnocentrism: Evolutionary Dimensions of Xenophobia, Discimination, Racism and Nationalism*. London: Croom Helm.

Armanazi, Ghayth. 1974. "The Rights of the Palestinians: The International Definition." In *Journal of Palestine Studies: A Quarterly on Palestinian Affairs and the Arab/Israeli Conflict* 111, no. 3. Beirut: Institute for Palestine Studies and Kuwait University.

Avery, Christopher L. 1983. "Refugee Status Decision-Making: The System of Ten Countries." *Stanford Journal of International Law* 19, no. 2.

Balogh, Elemer. 1943. *Political Refugees in Ancient Greece: From the Period of the Tyrants to Alexander the Great.* Johannesburg: Witwatersrant University Press.

Baron, Salo. 1983. *A Social and Religious History of the Jews.* Vol. 2, Late Middle Ages and Era of European Expansion 1200–1650. New York: Columbia University Press.

Basok, Tanya. 1988. "Local Settlement of Salvadoran Refugees in Costa Rica: Small Urban Enterprises." Ph.D. thesis, York University.

Bau, Ignatius. 1985. *This Ground is Holy: Church Sanctuary and the Central American Refugees.* New York: Paulist Press.

Bramwell, Anna C., ed. 1988. *Refugees in the Age of Total War.* London: Unwin Hyman.

Britton, Roswell S. 1935. "Chinese Interstate Intercourse Before 700 B.C."*The American Journal of International Law* 29.

Brubaker, William R. 1989. "Membership without Citizenship: The Economic and Social Rights of Non-citizens." In *Immigration and the Politics of Citizenship in Europe and North America,* edited by William R. Brubaker. New York: University Press of America.

Bulmerincq, August. [1853] 1970. *Das Asylrecht in seiner geschlichtlichen Entwicklung.* Wiesbaden: Dr. Martin Sandig.

Canadian Council for Refugees. 1993. *Report of Spring 1992 Consultation.*

Carens, Joseph. 1987a. "Aliens and Citizens: The Case for Open Borders." *The Review of Politics* 49, Spring.

——. 1987b. "Who Belongs? Theoretical and Legal Questions about Birthright Citizenship in the U.S." *University of Toronto Law Journal,* no. 37.

——. 1992. "Democracy and Respect for Difference: The Case of Fiji." *University of Michigan Journal of Law Reform,* 25, Spring–Summer.

——. Forthcoming. "The Rights of Immigrants." In *Group Rights,* edited by Judith Baker. Toronto: University of Toronto Press.

Carlisle, Richard, ed. 1990. *The Illustrated Encyclopedia of Mankind.* London: M. Cavendish.

Caroz, Ya-acob. 1975. "The Palestinians: Who Are They?" In *The Palestinians: People, History, Politics,* edited by Michael Curtis, Chaim Waxman, Joseph Neyer and Allen Pollack. New Jersey: Transaction Books.

Cervenka, Zdenek. 1979. *The Organization of African Unity and its Charter.* New York: F.A. Praeger.

Cohn, Haim H. 1984. *Human Rights in Jewish Law.* New York: KTAV Publishing House.

Communiqué. 1993, July 8. House of Commons, Ottawa.

Cox, J. Charles. 1911. *The Sanctuaries and Sanctuary Seekers of Medieval England.* London: George Allen and Sons.

Davis, John H. 1969. "The Palestine Refugee Problem." In *Selected Essays on the Palestine Question*, edited by Ibrahim ali-Abid. Beirut: Palestine Liberation Organization-Research Center.

Dowty, Alan. 1987. *Closed Borders.* New Haven: Yale University Press.

Dunbar, Robin I.M. 1987. Contributor to Reynolds, Falger, and Vine, eds., *The Sociobiology of Ethnocentrism: Evolutionary Dimensions of Xenophobia, Discrimination, Racism and Nationalism.* London: Croom Helm.

Elbright, Donald F. 1954. *Free India: The First Five Years.* Nashville, Tennesee: Parthenon Press.

Employment and Immigration Canada. 1993. "Consultations on Immigration." Ottawa: February–April, 1993.

Eriksson, L.G., G. Melander, and P. Nobel, eds. 1981. *An Analysing Account of the Conference on the African Refugee Problem.* Uppsala: Scandinavian Institute of African Studies.

Etzioni, Amitai. 1990. "Liberals and Communitarianism." In *Partisan Review* 2.

——. 1993. *The Spirit of Community: Rights, Responsibilities, and the Communitarian Agenda.* New York: Crown Publishers.

Falger, Vincent. 1987. Contributor to Reynolds, Falger, and Vine, eds., *The Sociobiology of Ethnocentrism: Evolutionary Dimensions of Xenophobia, Discrimination, Racism and Nationalism.* London: Croom Helm.

Frelick, Bill. 1992a. "Call Them What They Are—Refugees,"*World Refugee Survey.* U.S. Committee for Refugees.

——. 1992b. "Haiti: No Room at the Inn," in *Refugees*, no. 90. UNHCR, Geneva (September).

Gerety, Tom. 1988. "Sanctuary: A Comment on the Ironic Relation Between Law and Morality." In *The New Asylum Seekers: Refugee Law in the 1980s*, edited by David A. Martin. Dordrecht, Netherlands: Kluwar Academic Publishers.

Gibney, Mark, ed. 1988. *Open Borders? Closed Societies? The Ethical and Political Issues.* New York: Greenwood Press.

Glenn, H. Patrick. 1992. *Strangers at the Gate: Refugees, Illegal Entrants, and Procedural Justice.* Les Editions Yvon Blais Inc., Report for Employment and Immigration Canada.

Goodblatt, M.S. 1952. *Jewish Life in Turkey in the XVIth Century as reflected in the legal writings of Samuel De Medina.* New York: The Jewish Theological Seminary of America.

Goodwin-Gill, Guy S. 1988. "Non-Refoulement and the New Asylum Seekers." In *The New Asylum Seekers: Refugee Law in the 1980s*, edited by David A. Martin. Dordrecht, Netherlands: Kluwar Academic Publishers.

——. 1983. *Refugees in International Law.* Oxford: Oxford University Press.

Grahl-Madsen, Atle. 1985. *Territorial Asylum.* London: Oceania Publications, Inc.

——. 1985. *The Emergent International Law Relating to Refugees.* University of Bergen.

Hailbronner, Kay. 1989. "Citizenship and Nationhood in Germany." In *Immigration and the Politics of Citizenship in Europe and North America,* edited by William R. Brubaker. New York: University Press of America.

Hans, Asha. 1993. "Sri Lankan Tamil Refugees in India," *Refuge* 13, 3.

Hardin, Garrett. 1986. "Lifeboat Ethics: The Case against Helping the Poor." *Philosophical Issues in Human Rights: Theories and Applications,* edited by Patricia H. Werhane, A.R. Gini and David T. Ozar. New York: Random House.

Hathaway, James C. 1991.*The Law of Refugee Status.* Toronto: Butterworths.

——. 1993a (February) "The emerging politics of non-entrée," *Refugees,* 91. Geneva: UNHCR.

——. 1993b (May–June) "The Threat of European Integration,"*Compass.*

Hindley, Geoffrey. 1990. *The Book of Magna Carta.* London: Constable and Co.

Hodges, Tony. 1984a. "Africa's Refugee Crisis." *Africa Report,* 29, 1.

——. 1984b. "Interview: William R. Smyser—UN Deputy High Commissioner for Refugees." *Africa Report,* 29, 1.

Holborn, Louise W. 1975. *Refugees: A Problem of our Time.* Metuchen, NJ: Scarecrow Press, 1975.

Horwitz, Robert. 1990. Introduction to John Locke, *Questions Concerning the Law of Nature.* London: Cornell University Press.

Hossie, Linda. 1992, May 16. "Palestinians Assert Right of Return: Sensitive Issue Raised at Mideast Talks Despite Wishes of Canadian Hosts." *The Globe and Mail.*

Ike, Ben W. 1987. Contributor to Reynolds, Falger, and Vine, eds., *The Sociobiology of Ethnocentrism: Evolutionary Dimensions of Xenophobia, Discrimination, Racism and Nationalism.* London: Croom Helm.

Immigration Canada. 1993. *Immigration Consultations 1993.* Final Report. Ottawa.

Kang, Jian. 1992. Research paper on natural law in China, prepared for this study.

Kibreab, Gaim. 1985. *African Refugees: Reflections on the African Refugee Problem.* Trenton, N.J.: African World Press of the Africa Research and Publications Project, 1985.

——. 1989. *Journal of Refugee Studies,* 2, no. 40.

Kimminich, Otto. 1968. *Asylrecht.* Berlin: Hermann Luchterhand Verlag GmbH.

Kirkwood, K. 1987. Contributor to Reynolds, Falger, and Vine, eds., *The Sociobiology of Ethnocentrism: Evolutionary Dimensions of Xenophobia, Discrimination, Racism and Nationalism.* London: Croom Helm.

Lam, Lawrence. 1992. Talk on Comprehensive Plan of Action Conference for Boat People, December 1, York University.

Larkin, M. A., F.C. Cuny, and B.N. Stein. 1991. *Repatriation Under Conflict in Central America.* Georgetown University, Washington: Hemispheric Migration Project, Center for Immigration Policy and Refugee Assistance and Intertech Institute.

Leddy, Mary Jo. 1993 (May–June). "An Invitation to be Neighbours."*Compass.*

Levi, Rabbi John S. 1992. "Welcome Stranger." Address at the National Forum on Refugees. Melbourne, Australia, 21 June.

Levi, Rabbi John S., and G.F.J Bergman. 1974. *Australian Genesis: Jewish Convicts and Settlers, 1788–1850.* London: Hale.

Locke, John. 1965. *Essays on the Law of Nature.* Edited by W. von Leyden. Oxford: Clarendon Press.

Loescher, G., and J.A. Scanlan. 1986. *Calculated Kindness: Refugees and America's Half-Open Door, 1945 to the Present.* New York: Free Press.

Macalister-Smith, Peter. 1989. "Humanitarian Action and International Law." In *The Moral Nation: Humanitarianism and U.S. Foreign Policy Today,* edited by Bruce J. Nichols and Gil Loescher. Notre Dame, Indiana: University of Notre Dame Press.

MacIntyre, Alasdair C. 1988. *Whose Justice? Which Rationality?* Notre Dame: University of Notre Dame Press.

MacMillan, Leanne. 1993. "Reflections on the Gender Guidelines." *Refuge,* 13, no. 4.

Maritain, Jacques. 1958. *The Rights of Man.* London: Robert Maclehose, The University Press.

Marrus, Michael R. "Introduction" in *Refugees in the Age of Total War,* edited by Anna C. Bramwell. London: Unwin Hyman, 1988.

Martin, William A.P. 1901. *The Lore of Cathay, or The Intellect of China.* New York: Revell.

McConnell, Michael. 1989. "A View From the Sanctuary Movement." In *The Moral Nation: Humanitarianism and U.S. Foreign Policy Today,* edited by Bruce J. Nichols and Gil Loescher. Notre Dame, Indiana: University of Notre Dame Press.

McKinley, Brunson. 1992 (September). "U.S. Policy." *Refugees.* Geneva: UNHCR.

Melander, G., and P. Nobel, eds. 1979. "Conference on the Legal, Economic, and Social Aspects of African Refugee Problems, 9–18 October 1976."

International Legal Instruments on Refugees in Africa. Uppsala: Scandinavian Institute of African Studies.

Meyers, Diana T. 1985. *Inalienable Rights: A Defense.* New York: Columbia University Press.

Milgrom, Jacob. 1990. *The JPS Torah Commentary—Numbers.* Philadelphia: Jewish Publication Society.

Miller, Jake C. 1982. "The Homeless of Africa." *Africa Today* 29, no. 2.

Milligan, Charles S. 1989. "Ethical Aspects of Refugee Issues and U.S. Policy." In *Refugee Law and Policy: International and U.S. Responses,* edited by Ved P. Nanda. New York: Greenwood Press.

Nanda, Ved P., ed. *Refugee Law and Policy: International and U.S. Responses.* New York: Greenwood Press.

Nichols. Bruce J., 1988. *The Uneasy Alliance: Religion, Refugee Work, and U.S. Foreign Policy.* New York: Oxford University Press.

Nichols, Bruce J., and Gil Loescher. 1989. Introduction in *The Moral Nation: Humanitarianism and U.S. Foreign Policy Today,* edited by Bruce J. Nichols and Gil Loescher. Notre Dame, Indiana: University of Notre Dame Press.

Nickel, James W. 1983. "Human Rights and the Rights of Aliens." In *The Border that Joins,* edited by Peter G. Brown and Henry Shue. New Jersey: Rowman and Littlefield.

Nouwen, Henri J.M. 1974. "Hospitality" in *Monastic Studies,* no. 11. Pine City, N.Y.: Mount Saviour Monastery.

Ogata, Sadako. 1993 (April). *Refugees* . Geneva: UNHCR.

Osuna, J.P., and C.M. Hanson. 1993. "U.S. Refugee Policy: Where We've Been, Where We're Going?" *World Refugee Survey.* U.S. Committee for Refugees.

Otunnu, Ogenga. 1994. "Refugee Movements from the Sudan: An Overview Analysis." *Refuge* 13, no. 4.

Paine, Thomas. 1969. *Rights of Man.* Harmondsworth: Penguin.

Palumbo, Michael. 1982. *Human Rights: Meaning and History.* Malabar, Fla.: Robert Z. Krieger Publishing Co.

Peters, Joan. 1976. "An Exchange of Populations" in *Commentary* 6.

———. 1984. *From Time Immemorial: The Origins of the Arab-Jewish Conflict Over Palestine.* New York: Harper and Row.

Plaut, W. Gunther, ed. [1981] 1993. *The Torah—A Modern Commentary.* New York: Union of American Hebrew Congregations.

———. 1985 (July 31). *Refugee Determination in Canada, Part II. Issues and Questions.* A Report to the Honourable Flora MacDonald, Minister of Employment and Immigration.

Plender, Richard. 1989. "The Present State of Research Carried Out by the English-speaking Section of the Centre for Studies and Research." In *The Right of Asylum*. Centre for Studies and Research in International Law and International Relations, Hague Academy of International Law: Martinus Nijhoff Publishers.

Pritchard, James B. 1955. *Ancient Near Eastern Texts*. Princeton: Princeton University Texts.

Rahula, Walpola Sri. 1959. *What the Buddha Taught*. Rev. ed. New York: Grove Press.

Reaman, Elmore G. 1963. *The Trail of the Huguenots in Europe, the United States, South Africa, and Canada*. Toronto: Thomas Allen.

Refuge 13, no. 9. Special Issue on Integration of Refugees—The Canadian Experience.

Refugees. 1992. (September). "U.S. Policy." Geneva: UNHCR.

Reynolds, V., V. Falger, and I. Vine. 1987. *The Sociobiology of Ethnocentrism: Evolutionary Dimensions of Xenophobia, Discrimination, Racism and Nationalism*. London: Croom Helm.

Rose, S., L.J. Kamin, and R.C. Lewontin. 1984. *Not in Our Genes: Biology, Ideology, and Human Nature*. Harmondsworth: Penguin.

Rosenberg, M. B., and P.L. Shepherd, eds. 1986. *Honduras Confronts Its Future: Contending Perspectives on Critical Issues*. Boulder, Col.: Lynne Rienner Publishers.

Rubin, Gary E. 1991. "Babel and Beyond: Ethics, Opportunity and Power in a Multi-Cultural Society" (unpublished).

Saddhatissa, H. 1971. *The Buddha's Way*. London: George Allen and Unwin Ltd.

Sahai, Gouind. 1948. *Reception, Relief and Rehabilitation of Refugees in the United Provinces*. Lucknow: Sahitya Mandir Press Ltd.

Salhany, Roger E. 1986. *The Origin of Rights*. Toronto: Carswell.

Sandor, E., and G. Coty. 1968. *The Rights of Man: The Universal Declaration of Human Rights*. Sydney: F.W. Cheshire.

Schambeck, Herbert. 1974. "The Ethical and Moral Basis of Human Rights." In *Protection of Human Rights*. Geneva: World Health Organization for the International Organization of Medical Sciences.

Schuck, P. H., and R.M. Smith. 1985. *Citizenship without Consent: Illegal Aliens in the American Polity*. New Haven: Yale University Press.

Sen, Armatya. 1993 (April 8). "The Threats to Secular India," in *The New York Review of Books* .

Shack, W. A., and E.P. Skinner. 1979. *Strangers in African Societies*. Berkeley: University of California Press.

Shahin, Miriam. 1992, May 14. "Palestinians Adamant on Returning Home."
    The Globe and Mail.

Sherman, Charles Phineas. 1933. *Principles and Rules: Roman Readings in Roman
    Law.* New York: Baker, Voorhis and Co.

Shmuelevitz, Aryeh. 1984. *The Jews of the Ottoman Empire in the Late 15th and the
    16th Centuries: Administrative, Economic, Legal and Social Relations as re-
    flected in the Responsa.* Leiden, The Netherlands: E.J. Brill.

Shoa, Asfaha. 1988. "De l'érythrée." Ph.D. thesis. École des Hautes Études en
    Sciences Sociales.

Shue, Henry. 1986. "The Basic Rights of Security and Subsistence." In *Philo-
    sophical Issues in Human Rights: Theories and Applications,* edited by Patricia
    H. Werhane, A.R. Gini and David T. Ozar. New York: Random House.

———. 1989. "Morality, Politics, and Humanitarian Assistance." In *The Moral
    Nation: Humanitarianism and U.S. Foreign Policy Today,* edited by Bruce J.
    Nichols and Gil Loescher. Notre Dame, Indiana: University of Notre
    Dame Press.

Silverman, Irwin. 1987. Introduction to Reynolds, Falger, and Vine, eds. *The
    Sociobiology of Ethnocentrism: Evolutionary Dimensions of Xenophobia, Dis-
    crimination, Racism and Nationalism.* London: Croom Helm.

Singer, P., and R. Singer. 1988. "The Ethics of Refugee Policy." In *Open Borders?
    Closed Societies? The Ethical and Political Issues,* edited by Mark Gibney.
    New York: Greenwood Press.

Singh, Nagendra. 1984. *The Role and Record of the UN High Commissioner For
    Refugees.* New Delhi: Macmillan India Limited.

Sinha, Prakesh G. 1971. *Asylum and International Law.* The Hague: Martinus
    Nijhoff.

Smith, Rogers M. 1989. "Morality, Humanitarianism, and Foreign Policy: A
    Purposive View." In *The Moral Nation: Humanitarianism and U.S. Foreign
    Policy Today,* edited by Bruce J. Nichols and Gil Loescher. Notre Dame:
    University of Notre Dame Press.

Spiro, Melford E. 1982. *Buddhism and Society: A Great Tradition and Its Burmese
    Vicissitudes.* Berkeley: University of California Press.

Spring Consultation of the Canadian Council for Refugees, 1992.

Strouts, Hazel. 1992, August 8. "The life-boat dilemma." *The Globe and Mail.*

UNHCR. 1993. The State of the World's Refugees: The Challenge of Protection.
    Toronto: Penguin Books.

Tabori, Paul. 1972. The Anatomy of Exile. London: George G. Harrap and Co.

Takaaki, Mizuno. 1990 (January/March). "The Refugee Quandry." *Japan Quar-
    terly* 37.

Teitelbaum, Michael. 1980. "Right versus Right." *Foreign Affairs* 59.

Tichy, Roland. 1990. *Ausländer rein! Warum es kein "Ausländer Problem" gibt.* Munich and Zurich: Piper.

Thomas, Elbert Duncan. 1927. *Chinese Political Thought: A Study Based upon the Theories of the Principal Thinkers of the Chou Period.* New York: Prentice-Hall Inc.

Thomas, G., and M.M. Witts. 1974. *The Voyage of the Damned.* New York: Stein and Day.

Tomeh, George. 1975. "Legal Status of the Arab Refugees." In *The Palestinians: People, History, Politics,* edited by Michael Curtis, Chaim Waxman, Joseph Neyer and Allen Pollack. New Jersey: Transaction Books.

Trungpa, Chögyam. 1991. *The Heart of the Buddha.* Boston: Shambhaia.

UNHCR. 1993. *Collection of International Instruments Concerning Refugees.* Geneva: UNHCR.

United Nations. 1978. "The Right of Return of the Palestinian People." Committee on the Exercise of the Inalienable Rights of the Palestinian People. New York.

——. 1983. "Sustaining Afghan Refugees in Pakistan." Geneva.

——. 1984. "Afghan Refugees in Pakistan: From Emergency to Self-Reliance." Geneva.

——. 1990. "The Situation in the Middle East: A Report from the Secretary-General." General Assembly Security Council, 45th Session Agenda, Item 35, November 26.

——. 1991 (April). The Committee on the Exercise of the Inalienable Rights of the Palestinian People and the Division for Palestinian Rights. Information Note, Issue 6. New York.

U.S. Committee for Refugees. 1982 (December). "Afghan Refugees in Pakistan: Will They Go Home Again?" New York.

Van der Dennen, Johan M.G. 1987. Contributor to Reynolds, Falger, and Vine, eds., *The Sociobiology of Ethnocentrism: Evolutionary Dimensions of Xenophobia, Discrimination, Racism and Nationalism.* London: Croom Helm.

Villalpando, Waldo. 1991. "Asylum in History." In *Quaderni/An Instrument of Peace: For Forty Years, UNHCR Alongside Refugees,* edited by Lionello Boscardi, Antonella Gesulfo and Waldo Villalpando. UNHCR.

Walzer, Michael. 1983. *Spheres of Justice: A Defense of Pluralism and Equality.* New York: Basic Books.

Weiss, M. Charles. 1854. *History of the French Protestant Refugees.* New York: Stringer and Townsend.

Wensinck, A.J., and J.H. Kramers, eds. 1976. *Handwoerterbuch des Islam.* Leiden: E.J. Brill.

Werhane, P.H., A.R. Gini and D.T. Ozar, eds. 1986. *Philosophical Issues in Human Rights: Theories and Applications*. New York: Random House.

Westerflier, W.J.E.M. van Hovell tot. 1989. "Africa and Refugees: The OAU Refugee Convention in Theory and Practice." *Netherlands Quarterly of Human Rights* 7, no. 2.

Whitaker, E. 1992. "The Schengen Movement and Its Portent for the Freedom of Personal Movement in Europe." *Georgetown Immigration Law Journal*, 191.

Wilson, James Q. 1993. "What Is Moral and How Do We Know It." *Commentary* 95, no. 6.

Winter, Roger. 1984. "Refugee Protection in Africa: Current Trends." Paper presented at the Washington Institute for Values in Public Policy Conference on U.S. Policy Toward Africa, September 19.

Wipfler, William F. 1985. "Refugees and Human Rights." In *Sanctuary*, edited by Gary MacEoin. San Francisco: Harper and Row Publishers.

Wolff, Ernest. 1960. *Die Religion in Geschichte und Gegenwart*. Vol. 4.

World Refugee Survey. 1993. "Country Reports." U.S. Committee for Refugees.

Yasuhiki, Saito. 1990 (January/March). "Imposter Refugees, Illegal Immigrants." *Japan Quarterly* 37.

Zinzer, Adolfo Aquila. 1991. "Repatriation of Guatemalan Refugees in Mexico." In *Repatriation Under Conflict in Central America*, edited by Mary Ann Larkin, Frederick C. Cuny and Barry N. Stein. Washington: Georgetown University.

Zolberg, Aristide. 1993. Talk on history of nation states and refugees, July 8, York University.

Zolberg, A. R., A. Suhrke, and S. Aguayo. 1989. *Escape from Violence: Conflict and the Refugee Crisis in the Developing World*. New York: Oxford University Press.

Index

Legitimate and Illegitimate Discrimination:
New Issues in Migration

Edited by Howard Adelman

ISBN 1–55014–238–0. 1995. 287 pp., indexed. $22.95

Freedom of movements: If the members of a state are forced to flee, the legitimacy of that government is questionable. On the other hand, if members cannot or must leave, again the government is not democratically legitimate. Immigration control: While limiting access and determining who may or may not become members of a sovereign state remains a legitimate prerogative of the state, the criteria, rules and processes for doing so must be compatible with its character as a democratic state. *Legitimate and Illegitimate Discrimination: New Issues in Migration,* edited by Professor Howard Adelman, deals with the question of legitimacy with cases studies from the Developing World, Europe, Australia, and the United States.

CONTENTS: Legitimate Immigration Control (Rainer Bauböck); the Concept of Legitimacy Applied to Immigration (Howard Adelman); The African Refugee Regime with Emphasis on North-eastern Africa: The Emerging Issues (Gaim Kibreab); The Refugee Problem in West Africa: Some Responses to Legitimate and Illegitimate Migration (A. Essuman-Johnson); Definitions of Legitimacy: Afghan Refugees in Pakistan (Grant M. Farr); Hong Kong Chinese: Facing the Political Changes in 1997 (Lawrence Lam); New Directions in Migration: The Case of Peru (Oscar Schiappa-Pietra); Immigration Regulation: The Cost to Integration (Tomas Hammar); Immigration Légale ou Illégale: La Situation des Demandeurs d'Asile dans la France d'Aujourd'hui [the Legal Situation of Asylum-seekers in France (in French)] (Frédéric Tiberghien); New Issues in Migration: Case Study—Australia (Lois Foster); United States Immigration Policy: The Conflict Between Human Rights and Perceptions of National Identity and Self-Interest (Arthur C. Helton).

Refugee Rights:
Report on a Comparative Survey
James C. Hathaway and John A. Dent
ISBN 1–55014–266–6. 1995. 82 pp. $11.95

Are visa controls intended to keep refugees from reaching an asylum country legal? Can asylum-seekers legitimately contest conditions of detention? At what point do refugees have the right to work, or to claim social assistance?

These are among the many issues addressed by *Refugee Rights: Report on a Comparative Survey,* a ground-breaking analysis of the human rights of refugees around the world. Working in collaboration with thirty renowned legal experts from Europe, Africa, Asia, Oceania, North America, and Latin America, Professor James Hathaway, Osgoode Hall Law School, and John Dent, Refugee Law Unit, Centre for Refugee Studies, York University, analyze the international legal instruments that set the human rights of refugees. By grounding their analysis in real-life challenges facing refugees today, Hathaway and Dent have produced a book as valuable to activists as to scholars.

Refugee Rights will provoke debate on the adequacy of the international refugee rights regime. It is essential reading for everyone concerned to counter threats to the human dignity of refugees.

Refuge

Refuge—Canada's periodical on refugees, founded in 1981 as a quarterly, is now published ten times a year by the Centre for Refugee Studies, York University. It publishes scholarly articles that inform the public about refugee issues. Covering current topics and providing updated statistics, *Refuge* provides a forum to discuss issues such as refugee status determination, sponsorship, and ongoing resettlement needs and programs. Submissions on these and other related issues are welcome for publication consideration in *Refuge*.

Friends of the Centre for Refugee Studies who donate $75 or more to the Centre receive Canadian income tax receipts from York University and courtesy copies of *Refuge*. An index, complete sets of *Refuge*, or individual copies are available.

Refuge subscription rates (one year - ten issues):
Canada $50; All other countries U.S.$60.

Please send your subscription requests to:

Managing Editor, York Lanes Press
Suite 351, York Lanes, Centre for Refugee Studies
York University, North York, Ontario Canada M3J 1P3
Tel: (416) 736–5663 • Fax: (416) 736–5837
Internet: refuge@vm1.yorku.ca